"My good friend Ron Simmons has written brilliantly on the path to success in *Life Lessons from the Little Red Wagon*. As Ron's pastor, I have watched this man live his faith, lead his family, and love his God both in the public and private arenas. This is a book filled with real-life wisdom and inspiring faith. Let Ron take you for a ride in the little red wagon. It just might change your life."

—**DR. JACK GRAHAM,** Senior Pastor,
Prestonwood Baptist Church

"Ron Simmons's book *Life Lessons from the Little Red Wagon* will be a game-changer for so many readers given his tremendous success in business and politics. His folksy style makes for an entertaining read. Most of all, the book is an inspiration for each of us to keep the right perspective on the right priorities in life."

—**DR. KEVIN ROBERTS,** President,
The Heritage Foundation

"I have known and loved Ron Simmons for decades. His reputation is spotless, and his character is beyond reproach, which brings tremendous legitimacy to this intriguing and innovative book on leadership. Ron is a leader—at home, in the office, and in government. Wherever you find him he rises to the top and always with well-deserved respect. Climb into this "little red wagon," grab hold of the handle, you are in for a great ride. Read it . . . and reap!"

—**O. S. HAWKINS,** Former Pastor, First Baptist
Church (Dallas), Author of the Bestselling
Code Series of Devotionals including *Bible Code*
and *Promise Code*

"Weaving heartfelt, personal storytelling with applicable wisdom, *Life Lessons from the Little Red Wagon* reads like a letter from a trusted mentor. Simmons offers his own setbacks and successes as a backdrop for an incredibly effective guide to personal and professional fulfillment. As a beneficiary of my dad's advice over the years, I can assure you: you'll be happy you've taken his words to heart."

—ALLIE BETH (SIMMONS) STUCKEY,
Host, *Relatable* Podcast and Author of
You're Not Enough and That's Okay

"*Life Lessons from the Little Red Wagon* outlines the life lessons the author learned throughout his career and details his Horatio Alger story on how he overcame great obstacles from growing up poor in Arkansas to achieving great success as both a businessman and politician."

—BILL QUINN, Founder and CEO (retired),
American Beacon Advisors

"My good friend and former colleague Ron Simmons is a great American and an exceptional human being! He has utterly nailed it with this book of great insights, heartwarming stories, and challenges for the reader! This book is a must-read, and I promise you it will be one you read again."

—THE HONORABLE PATRICK FALLON,
US Congressman–TX

"Ron paints a beautiful picture of how life and success actually work. Through simple lessons, he weaves together how to take charge of your life to create a legacy bigger than yourself. A must-read for anyone who desires more out of life and is ready to get comfortable with being uncomfortable!"

—GREG SINDELAR, CEO,
Texas Public Policy Foundation

"Using the acronym A.C.T. (Action, Consider, Takeaway), Ron leads the reader on a purposeful journey to create a life and family plan, regardless of their situation. Ron's analogy of his Radio Flyer childhood wagon is an excellent way to describe all the moving parts of life and their role in guiding the wagon forward in a positive direction, always keeping in mind all the wagons in your life (financial, family, spiritual, and career) and the roles they play in determining the outcome of the path you choose regardless of your circumstances. A must-read for everyone!"

—JAMES BALL. ED.D., B.C.B.A.-D.-LBA,
President and CEO,
JB Autism Consulting, LLC

"Books give us the capacity to acquire knowledge from others. Ron's experiences allow us to learn from his success and how to face life's inevitable challenges with courage and perseverance."

—CONGRESSMAN MICHAEL C.
BURGESS, M.D.

LIFE LESSONS
from the
LITTLE RED WAGON

LIFE LESSONS
from the
LITTLE RED WAGON

*15 Ways to Take Charge and
Create a Path to Success*

Hon. Ronald E. Simmons

with DON YAEGER

Foreword by JOHN C. MAXWELL

MAXWELL
LEADERSHIP

Published by Maxwell Leadership Books, an imprint of Forefront Books.

Distributed by Simon & Schuster.

Library of Congress Control Number: 2022921042

Print ISBN: 979-8-88710-004-3
E-book ISBN: 979-8-88710-005-0

Cover Design by Bruce Gore, Gore Studio, Inc.
Interior Design by Bill Kersey, KerseyGraphics

This book is dedicated to my wonderful wife, Lisa, who has shared almost every step of my journey without ever making me feel that I did not have her love and support—no matter how many uncomfortable steps we had to take. Also to my children, Justin, Daniel, and Allie Beth, who, with their different personalities, have taught me so much about peace, perseverance, and passion. Thank you, and I love you.

Contents

John C. Maxwell

*E*verything worthwhile in life is uphill. If something has value, the journey to achieving it is an uphill battle all the way to the top. Nobody accidentally climbed a mountain. We all have to work to get to higher ground.

That has certainly been true for Ron Simmons. I remember talking to him many years ago when he felt stuck in life. Ron was a successful businessman but wondered if there was something more out there for him. I encouraged Ron to take some time to reflect so that he could determine how to transition from success to significance. What came out of that time was Ron's decision to go into public service. He became highly intentional and worked to make a difference.

You can learn from Ron's story. Ron is just a regular guy who decided he wasn't going to settle in life. He has taken his ordinary life and gathered some pretty extraordinary ideas and thoughts, and he's put them into this book.

In some ways, Ron's story isn't so different from mine. I grew up in rural Ohio the son of a pastor and a librarian. Ron grew up in rural Arkansas the son of public school teachers. But because of the solid values Ron embraced and applied to his life, his dreams have come to fruition. So can yours.

This book provides principles anyone can follow. Comparing his journey to that of a kid with a little red wagon, he inspires desire, growth, and intentionality. Apply these lessons to your life and see where your journey takes you.

John C. Maxwell

CHAPTER 1

Finding Your Place in the Red Wagon

*A*s I pulled my Radio Flyer up the big hill near our house in Little Rock, Arkansas, I beamed with a new sense of freedom. The wagon wasn't shiny by any means. The red paint had lost some of its sheen, and the black rubber wheels were worn. I had received the wagon as a hand-me-down from my older brother, but I didn't see it that way. It was the mid-1960s and having something with wheels on it was pretty cool for a six-year-old. It indicated a big step in maturity, and I was happy to have it. I remember riding in it and pulling my toys around the neighborhood. I also had a sense of independence, which is what led me to the top of the hill. When I reached the peak, I aimed the red wagon toward the bottom, jumped inside, and shifted my weight to begin the descent. I learned a valuable lesson that day. As the wagon began rolling down the hill, the front wheels sputtered back and forth, shifting left and right. I was just a passenger, thinking the wagon would stay straight and provide a joyous ride to the bottom. All of a sudden, the wagon flipped over.

Thud! My chin hit the pavement, and the wagon went rolling.

I didn't realize it then, but my adventures in that red wagon would shape the way I would live my life. I learned that my little wagon had turned over because it didn't have anybody steering it. There I was, the wagon's cargo, whipping down the hill with increasing velocity—but without direction. Isn't that a lot like life? I don't know that I learned my lesson that day, which the bumps and bruises throughout my childhood would indicate, but the red wagon became my guide. Looking back over my life, I realize that for certain seasons I needed to have my hand on the handle. I was in charge of the steering, and I decided where to go and what to do. At other times, I wasn't in charge. I was part of the cargo, being pulled along by someone else. Some of the time it wasn't even my wagon at all. It belonged to a friend or coworker or family member. My job wasn't to steer; my job was to push. I didn't get (nor was I looking for) the credit. Rather, I was pushing from behind with all I had in me. It's amazing how something so simple—a box with four wheels and a handle—could become a gateway to adventure and opportunity, but that's just what my little red wagon did. It turns out that there are a lot of parallels to life, and whether yours is the great adventure it's meant to be depends on how your wagon is loaded, who's pulling on the handle, and who's helping you on your journey. No matter where you are in life, you can find yourself occupying one of the wagon's positions—the handle, front wheels, rear wheels, cargo, or the pusher. The people who are most effectively living their lives are willing to shift and pivot to whatever position moves the wagon forward.

I remember taking my daughter, Allie Beth, hunting near our countryside home when she was eight years old. We had been hunting for some time without much luck when Allie spoke up. "Dad, what are we doing?" she asked, frustrated. "Well, sweetheart," I told her, "they call it hunting, because we're looking." Allie was a pretty outspoken child and quipped, "I just call this a nature walk."

What I've learned in my life is that an empty wagon really is just a nature walk. You can sit in the wagon and steer it like I did that day on the hill in Arkansas, but you're not leading. You're sitting in the wagon holding the handle back, going downhill directionless. A wagon doesn't have any use unless there's cargo. What worth are the wagon, the wheels, and the leader pulling the handle if they aren't carrying something? Sometimes in life you're carrying your kids, sometimes you're carrying your faith, sometimes you're carrying others, and sometimes you're the one being carried.

By the time I was a teenager I knew I didn't want the ordinary life I had seen my parents live. There was nothing wrong with the path they chose, but I wanted something different. I felt like I had been part of a family that had been stuck in the rut of financial mediocrity for a while. It wasn't that they weren't good people or weren't doing good things, but financially, they struggled. That became my driving force. Even though I eventually ran two highly successful investment-advisory firms, I didn't grow up with any particular passion or dreams of being an investment advisor. I just knew I didn't want the copy-and-paste, drifting lifestyle. I had seen firsthand that financial mediocrity was no way to live. It didn't matter to me how I got there, I just needed to get there. If you aren't intentional about where you want to go in life and how you're going to get there, you'll end up in a rut of the status quo. So you've got to decide. The world is filled with people who live in conflict with that question all the time. They blame other people or situations. Certainly, there are plenty of obstacles in life, but what it often comes down to is people not being willing to make the hard decision or ask the next uncomfortable question.

That's what I have always admired about Dr. Ben Carson. He grew up in inner-city Detroit, raised by a mother with a third-grade education who had never learned to read. His parents divorced when he was eight, and his family lived off food stamps. Carson could have settled for the ordinary, and the world would have known no different, but he aspired for more. He dreamed of becoming a doctor and battled through adversity to earn a scholarship to Yale. In 1984, and still in his early thirties, Carson was named Director of Pediatric Neurosurgery at Johns Hopkins. In 2008, he received the Presidential Medal of Freedom, the highest honor bestowed to an American civilian. If Carson had listened to what everybody else was saying, those accomplishments would have been impossible. But he refused to let anyone else determine what his journey looked like. He grabbed the handle and decided where he was going and how he was going to get there.

Navigating life's journey has its challenges, but the person in front leading the wagon determines the path forward. They see opportunity and danger, but each step guides the wagon in the proper direction toward its destination.

One of the things my wife, Lisa, and I taught our three children is that you have to decide what's important to you in life and determine, "What path do I have to take to accomplish that?" I was probably thirteen when that question first crossed my mind. *How do I get on a different path?* I wondered. Along the way, there were different routes I could take that would lead me in a new direction. Those were decisions I had to make.

Sometimes you just have to take the handle.

It Begins with a Dream

In 1914, a sixteen-year-old boy from Venice, Italy, armed with nothing more than the carpentry skills he learned from his father and grandfather and a vision of the American Dream, set his sights on a better life. He had a cousin living in Chicago so his parents sold the family's mule to pay for his one-way ticket, and he boarded a ship that would carry him thousands of miles across the Atlantic Ocean into New York Harbor.

When Antonio Pasin arrived at Ellis Island on April 19, 1914, there was nothing about him indicating he would be successful in the future. He exited the ship that day with no money and no job. All he had was the hope for a better life than the one he left behind. When Pasin reached Chicago, his youth made it hard to find a job. Unwilling to accept defeat, Pasin found small jobs—washing vegetables and hauling water for a sewer-digging crew—to save money for woodworking equipment. By 1917, Pasin had saved enough to rent a one-room workshop, where he used his carpentry skills to build phonograph cabinets day and night. To carry his cabinets to local shops, Pasin built a small wooden wagon. As he went around from store to store, customers started taking interest in the wagon. He nicknamed his wooden wagon the Liberty Coaster after the Statue of Liberty that had welcomed him to the country. With its wooden cargo box, steel-rimmed wheels, and T-shaped handle, its simplicity was its brilliance.

In 1923, Pasin launched the Liberty Coaster Company and watched orders for his wooden wagons take off. By 1927, Pasin realized he needed to make a change to meet demand, so he adopted the mass-production techniques pioneered by Henry Ford. That, combined with stamping new metal wagon bodies, allowed him to accept and fulfill an order for seven thousand wagons. That year, Pasin changed the name of the company to Radio Flyer, inspired by fellow Italian Guglielmo Marconi's pioneering radio transmission and Charles Lindbergh's flight across the Atlantic Ocean. Like these great men, and unbeknownst to him at the time, Pasin himself had become a pioneer.

Pasin's little red wagon became an important part of childhood for so many, providing a vehicle for the whims of countless childhood imaginations. We could pretend it was a spaceship or race car. We could pull our toys or push our friends. The Radio Flyer became synonymous with the hope and optimism of childhood, the great equalizer for every walk of American life. During the Great Depression, Radio Flyer continued to make 1,500 red wagons each day. Even in those challenging times, the red wagon provided hope. Today, more than one hundred million Radio Flyer wagons have been sold. I've pulled my children and grandchildren in one version of a Radio Flyer or another, and today I see it as so much more than a metal wagon.

We remember our red wagons for the adventures they ingrained in our memories and for the moments when our parents pulled us along on those summer days. But I also remember my Radio Flyer for the life lessons it taught—including the hard one forced on me as I tumbled down the hill at six years old. Today I see the little red wagon as the perfect metaphor for life and the decisions that guide our everyday journeys. In life, there are pushers and pullers, wheels that determine our life's direction and provide momentum, the important cargo we carry, and the handle that guides the way. All are important, but at different times in life our role changes.

I've always said, it's easy to leave behind an empty wagon. Each day we're tasked with carrying so many important components from one destination to the next. It might be our family or faith. Sometimes it's our work or finances. And, as you will learn later, sometimes it's your community, state, or country. No matter what our cargo is, every wagon needs someone to take the handle and pull or it doesn't move. When Pasin left Italy for America, he did so with a plan and a determination to overcome anything that stood in his way. It was the vision that led a sixteen-year-old boy to chart a new course for generations that followed.

Creating a New Path in Life

There was nothing special about me that said I should have been successful. There were no indicators in my early years that pointed to me being a cofounder of an investment business that would grow from zero clients to $3 billion under management or being involved in decisions affecting a state that, were it a sovereign nation, would be the tenth-largest economy in the world. Seriously, there was nothing!

I was born in Baton Rouge, Louisiana, but I spent my formative years in Junction City, Arkansas, the southernmost city in the state and where Stateline Road divides Arkansas from Louisiana. I could stand there and throw a rock across the border! It was a tiny town of 749 people when we moved there in 1973. At that time, I was a small-town twelve-year-old boy with an ordinary life. I didn't start out with anything. My mom and dad were public school teachers, divorced when I was in high school, and I paid my way through college, squeezing four years of college into ten. While my ancestors immigrated to America in the 1600s and built successful lives, basically everything was lost as a result of the Civil War. For a family that had been in America for hundreds of years, nothing stood out about us. Early on in my life, as I saw the way my family scraped by and watched my parents' marriage fall apart, I knew I wanted to take a different path and create a better future.

You might be reading this thinking, *Well, what was it? Why didn't you end up worse or the same? What was it that broke the cycle of mediocrity?* To be honest, I believe there are millions of people out there just like me. Maybe you're one of them. There are so many people who, through their family situations or their upbringing, see nothing that indicates they are going to break that cycle. Unlike Thomas Edison, Steve Jobs, and Mark Cuban, I didn't pull myself out of the rut with one big idea that changed the world. My journey wasn't like that. I've simply taken the next uncomfortable step for five-plus decades, and along the way I've been able to build a pretty successful life in all the ways that matter.

That's why it was so important for me to share my story and the lessons I've learned from the little red wagon. I don't think my life is very hard to emulate. There are a lot more Ron Simmonses in the world than there are Edisons, Jobses, and Cubans.

I didn't understand it as it was happening. But as I look back, I realize there were paths I had to choose, steps I had to take, and decisions I had to make. Whether it was moving out of my parents' house after high school, getting married when I was nineteen, leaving the comforts of a small town for a big city, or walking away from a job and millions of dollars, I had to decide. I made the decision that I wanted to put a stop to my family's legacy of mediocrity. But it wasn't like there was an epiphany. It was one uncomfortable, yet intentional, decision at a time, some bad and some good ones. Whatever you want, you have to be intentional about getting it.

Here's my mantra: if you're in your twenties you should be figuring out what you want to do with your life. Where do you want to go? Your thirties are all about moving yourself forward, gaining expertise and perfecting your craft. That might be in your personal life, spiritual life, or career. In your forties, it's time to become a leader. And people in their fifties should take all of that stuff and do something with exponential value. Don't say you'll do something later, and don't just drift through life hoping something will come your way. You'll never know when the bell tolls for you, and you can't plan your life banking on luck.

As I look back, there was definitely a road map that I followed. There were pushers and pullers who were important to me as I made my way through life and sometimes needed help out of the mud. Are you looking to pave a new path? If I can do it, so can you. Changing your direction can change your destination.

Building Your Red Wagon Journey

There is no exact road map to success or a happier life. Most people would say to be successful you need to go to a good college and get a degree, have some family success, and wait until after college to get married. I didn't check any of those boxes. While all of those things may have an impact on your future, none of them is a determinant. They might have made things easier, but not having those things didn't stop me. What I want you to understand is that there is no guaranteed formula for success, and there is no one-size-fits-all life.

The thing about the little red wagon is it doesn't go on its own, and without all the parts you'll never get where you want to go, whether in your business life, family life, spiritual life, or financial life. Each part of the wagon plays a very specific role and is critical to moving you forward. When all the parts work together, the results are undeniable.

The Handle. The handle determines the direction the wagon will go so only someone with clear vision should take hold of it. Since the first step forward is the one who sets the direction, it's critical that the handle knows where it's going. When you have control of the handle, you have to keep your eyes open for the road ahead. Sometimes the person pulling the handle is you, but in my life, a lot of times somebody else was pulling the handle. Whoever is leading the way is out front and sees things others can't. Whether it's opportunity or danger ahead, the puller determines the fate of the rest of the wagon and must be ready to make decisions and adjust the direction. Without the handle, you'd be forced to push the wagon, and the wheels would go one way or another, forcing the wagon off course.

The Front Wheels. Somewhere on your journey you're going to have to make adjustments. *Plans are made in sand; goals are made in concrete.* The front wheels are the only ones that can go left or right, and they ultimately determine your path. They carry out the leader's direction and are the first to realize a course correction. However, they can't move toward the goal on their own and are effective only if they're moving in the same direction. To get to your goals, there are going to be curves and bumps in the road, and when you change course, the front wheels communicate the change to the rest of the wagon, "Hey, we've got to change plans, but we're still going to get to our goal."

The Rear Wheels. The job of the rear wheels is to provide the energy and fuel for you to push the wagon forward. The rear wheels are your fundamentals and represent the daily grind of activity that moves you toward your goals. They're the boring, unsexy stuff that nobody loves to do, but they're critical to reaching your dreams. They only roll forward and backward and follow the front wheels. They don't think; they just trust the direction. The wagon could be headed off a cliff and they wouldn't know. But without the rear wheels the cargo would be dragging, our life would be dragging. Rear wheels on a wagon and in life are vital, every step of the way. They can wear out without regular lubrication, which in life is encouragement.

The Pusher. Sometimes in life we have to let somebody else lead the way. As the pusher, your whole job is to keep your eyes on the path ahead and push the wagon forward, allowing somebody else to see the vision and control the direction. Sometimes you won't even know your destination. A lack of effort kills momentum for everyone, so if the pusher isn't really pushing, the mission loses power. It requires patience so you don't outrun the leader and are prepared for a change in direction. It's difficult for those who are used to providing vision and direction to take on the role of pusher, but the sooner one recognizes that he is now filling the role of pusher, the better off everyone else involved with the journey will be.

The Cargo. Whether it's your family, financial situation, or work life, everybody has cargo they carry. It could be the choices you've made or your hopes and dreams for the future. The weight of the cargo is critical. Sometimes the payload can feel like a million pounds, can slow you down, and sometimes it gets stuck so you can't move at all. Be careful what you load yourself down with. Sometimes in life, you are the cargo, being guided by another person in your life or maybe even God.

As we pull our wagon, every step we take and decision we make can significantly alter our direction. In training, pilots are taught the 1 in 60 rule, which says that every one degree an airplane goes off course results in a sixty-mile detour. When we lose direction in life, it can take us off track and lead to unexpected outcomes. But just as easily as we can veer off track, a small change in direction can put us back on a better path. Just as our success is not predetermined, our mistakes are not unfixable. You have to be willing to find your right place in the wagon, and it's not always holding on to that handle. Sometimes even a puller isn't enough to move a heavily loaded wagon. That's when you need a pusher, that person in the back with two hands outstretched, giving all he or she has to move the wagon another inch forward. An important lesson I've learned is, you don't always have to be the puller. If you try to be the puller all the time, you're going to fail. So many people in life always want to be at the front of the line, but it's hard to learn best when you're always leading the way. And you don't always need to pull or push; sometimes you need to crawl inside the wagon and let someone else guide the way.

I was fifty-one years old when I ran for office in the Texas House of Representatives. I had already been CEO and chairman of an investment company with billions of dollars under management, but I had never been in politics. As I began my foray into the political world, I had to jump in the wagon and be the cargo so I could learn. I told my political consultant, "Tell me exactly what to do and I will do it." After a while, I jumped out of the wagon, went to the back, and started pushing. Even though I was fifty-one, I had become a pusher again. I don't care how successful you've been, you've got to be willing to take your place at any part of the wagon at any time depending on what is called for in your current circumstances.

Where are you now? Are you looking for pushers and pullers in your life? Sometimes they're there and, if you're not looking, you won't know it. They'll come and go, and you'll miss your opportunity. A lot of times during my life my next step seemed pretty clear, but I think it was because I was always seeking it. God, for whatever reason, gave me the desire to always look for mentors in my life, people who made me a bit uncomfortable. But those are the people who made me better. We could spend all our time with people who are at our level or below it, and we'd enjoy ourselves, but we wouldn't get any better. Your life is yours to create. What's your path going to be? Can you envision your horizon?

Whether you feel stuck and need a new path forward or are on track but are ready for the next challenge in life, the little red wagon can take you where you want to go.

Jump inside and let's get started.

~ *Chapter 1* ~
A.C.T. (Action, Consider, Takeaway)

Action

List all of your current wagons (financial, family, spiritual, career, and so forth).

Consider

Where are you, right now, in each of those wagons? Is that where you should be?

Takeaway

Be honest with yourself and position yourself in the right place in each wagon for today.

CHAPTER 2

Expecting the Unexpected

*T*he highway's center lines darted past in the rearview mirror of my 2014 black Chevrolet Silverado as I zoomed down US Highway 64 on the last leg of my trip from our home in Dallas to our cabin in Cashiers, North Carolina, near the Blue Ridge Mountains. As I drove in solitude, I couldn't ditch the burning question that filled my mind. *Did it really mean that much to you, Ron?*

A few weeks earlier, on November 6, 2018, I woke up on Election Day seeking my fourth term as the representative for District 65 in the Texas House of Representatives. When I ran for public office in 2012, I didn't want to serve forever. I always said that six years is enough for anybody and had planned to run for three terms at most. But politics aren't always cut-and-dried, and a change in the Texas Speaker of the House led me to decide to run one final time in 2018. In the days leading up to the election, my team and I felt good about my chances. In all our polling, we thought I'd win reelection for a fourth term by seven or eight points. That morning, I began making my way to the sixteen polling locations across my district, spending thirty minutes at each stop to be around my constituents before heading home to freshen up in anticipation of the polls closing at 7 p.m. A few minutes before the polls closed, I jumped in my Silverado and started on my drive to the Republican victory party. Around 7:02 p.m., the Republican county chair called. "Ron," she asked, "do you want the results of early voting and mail-in ballots?"

When the polls close in Texas, the tally for the early voting is released immediately. I knew from my first three elections that you generally know who is going to win from that initial release. It's hard to overcome a reasonable lead if you're behind in early voting. I didn't hesitate. "Sure," I told her, confident in our polling. I was stunned as she read off the early numbers. I was behind by two hundred votes! *Goodness, gracious*, I thought. I turned my truck around and called my wife, Lisa. "I'm coming home, sweetheart," I told her. She was just as shocked as I was.

When I got home we spent the night following the results on the Internet, and they didn't get any better. They worsened. I ended up losing by 1,327 votes out of some sixty thousand cast. I found the phone number for my Democratic opponent and called to congratulate her and offer my support with the transition.

The day after my defeat I drove around Denton County collecting my signs from different locations. Everybody was in shock. My staff, political consultant, friends in the House of Representatives, and family couldn't believe it. Losing that race was easily the most devastating thing I've ever experienced. I rarely lost in life, and the failure of losing that political race was personally hurtful. What happened after that was even more disturbing. Even more than losing, I was disappointed that losing *bothered me so much*.

As I said, when I started in politics I had planned on serving only three terms. I didn't guarantee it, but I thought that was enough. I had served for six years and accomplished many of the things I wanted. I'd done my time. And yet losing was devastating. I thought I could walk away from it at any time. I never realized my identity was so tied up in being an elected official. I was shocked at how much I had emotionally and soulfully invested in it and how much of an idol public service had become. Maybe God was showing me, "Ron, you got a little bit too caught up in this." He just reminded me a little more harshly than I thought he should! I don't think I was ever arrogant about it; I just enjoyed it so much that I probably neglected other, more important things without even realizing it.

A few weeks later, in early December 2018, the loss was still eating at me. I knew I needed to get away. "Hey," I told Lisa, "I'm going to the mountains." Lisa knew it was a good idea. I needed to be by myself and think about my future, to reflect on what the loss meant for me, and to understand *why I was so disappointed that I was disappointed.*

I'm privileged to call leadership expert John C. Maxwell a friend, and I'll never forget having a conversation with John before I got into politics. I was in my early fifties wondering, *Where do I go from here? What do I do?* I've always been a person who enjoys being busy. I'm not a sit-around guy. John encouraged me to just take time out of my day to think. It sounds so simple, but John was right. For so many of us, our lives are so busy that we never stop to think about all those great ideas we have or the ways we can solve our problems. John wrote in his book *Thinking for a Change: 11 Ways Highly Successful People Approach Life and Work*, "Your life today is a result of your thinking yesterday. Your life tomorrow will be determined by what you think today." What I learned from John is that successful people think differently, they remove distractions from their life, and they focus on what's truly important.

Ever since that conversation, I've tried to take time to think about life, whether I'm on the road by myself or sitting in a parking lot. It's important to just settle into thinking and not necessarily know what you're going to think about. Something will come to your mind. Maybe God's been trying to prompt you with it, and you've been too busy doing other stuff and haven't taken time to deal with it. It might be about an issue with a family member or a career decision you'll never solve because you never take time to stop and think. That's a big part of where you fit in the little red wagon at any point in your life. If you're always the person holding on to the handle, you're never going to garner the wisdom it takes to truly be the leader you need to be. Sometimes you need to be in other parts of the wagon. It's not always pleasant, but it's just the way it is. As my disappointment lingered, I needed to decompress and find out why losing had affected me so much.

I knew my loss didn't affect my financial well-being, it didn't affect my relationship with my family, it didn't affect my health, and it didn't affect my salvation. Of the things in life that are truly important, it didn't make any difference. But it really, really bothered me. Sometimes in life, especially when you've had a run of successes, a bump in the road throws you off your path. As I began my self-evaluation, I realized I wasn't infallible. I heard clearly, "Ron, there is a God." That's the good news. The bad news is, "He's not you!" After I told Lisa about my road trip, I set out on a ten-day pilgrimage to the mountains to find answers. How was I going to handle the disappointment going forward? Was I going to be bitter or was I going to be better?

The Lead-up to the Loss

I had a two-day drive ahead of me when I set out on my nearly one-thousand-mile trip from Dallas to Cashiers, North Carolina. I headed east on Interstate 20 toward Louisiana and started to think. My introspection began as it so often does in life's defeats. In those first hours on the road, I thought about the things that maybe I could have done differently. Everybody had been telling me, "There's no way you're gonna lose." What could I have done to change the outcome?

When I first decided to run for public office, I learned quickly that my big competition was in the Republican primary. When I got to the general election, it wasn't supposed to be any competition at all. My first Democratic opponent in 2012 spent less than $5,000 and still received nearly 40 percent of the vote. That always stuck with me. People didn't even know the guy; they just voted for him because of his party and the "D" next to his name. Texas allowed one-punch, straight-ticket voting, meaning someone could go into the voting booth, say they were going to vote Democratic or Republican, and the computer would automatically vote for every Democrat or Republican on the ballot. In that first election, my opponent didn't have to campaign, he didn't have to do anything, and he had nearly 40 percent of the vote with one push of a button. *We're going to get some pretty bad people in office*, I thought. As some urban counties started turning blue, there was a complete turnover in judges, from Republican to Democrat, in Texas. Some of the judges probably should have lost, but most judges aren't partisan and many were good judges. Partisan politics aside, it was clear straight-ticket voting was a problem.

Most states had already abolished straight-ticket voting when I brought a bill that would ban the practice in Texas to the floor of the House of Representatives in 2017. Similar bills had come and gone in Texas in the early 2000s, but they garnered little support. There wasn't much confidence from the outside that my bill would pass either. Still, I worked hard, got all the stakeholder groups together, and earned support from the Speaker of the House. It was a hard battle, but the bill eventually passed the House, 88–57. In Texas, bills that are passed generally become effective the next September. But when the bill made it to the Senate, they changed the effective date to September 2020, after the 2018 election. I was passionate about the bill. To ensure it passed, I went along with the change in effective date. In my previous three elections, the race between me and my Democratic opponents was getting progressively tighter. My opponents weren't spending much money, but people were voting straight-ticket based on the name at the top of the ballot, and it trickled down to my race. I knew if I ran for a fourth time it absolutely could get close, but I didn't think I'd lose. The irony was the delay in the effective date of the bill I passed to get rid of one-punch voting cost me my seat.

The reason it did was because, around that same time, it was announced that Robert Francis "Beto" O'Rourke would be running for US Senate against the junior senator from Texas, Ted Cruz. Because it wasn't a presidential election year, that US Senate battle would be at the top of the ticket. Beto was like Elvis Presley. He was charismatic, and young people flocked to him. I had learned through my time in politics that nothing is assured. You have to expect the unexpected. That's really important on any journey because something can derail you pretty easily. You have to realize there are things that are going to come up. They might be great, but they might be moments that challenge you. How you react to the unexpected determines what type of character you have. I certainly haven't always responded as I should, but it's a lesson that I continue to try to focus on. O'Rourke had thrown an unknown at our campaign, but we were still optimistic. I continued to work as hard as I had before and kept knocking on doors. When we did our polling, we still felt good.

On Election Day, Cruz won his Senate seat back but lost most of the suburban areas as Beto racked up votes. People went into the voting booths and just punched for the Democrat without considering the race for House District 65. Even though I beat Cruz in my district by ten points, I didn't have enough to overcome the Beto Effect. You start second-guessing after a loss like that. Maybe we should have done more of a comparison between my opponent and me. In reality, none of that mattered. People just went into the booth and hit the "D." (I'll share more insights about the 2018 election in chapter 14.)

What I learned from that race was that sometimes the plans in life are bigger than you. In this case, God's plan was obviously bigger than me. There wasn't any reason I should have lost that race. We didn't do anything particularly wrong. I didn't know it then, but I was just the cargo in the little red wagon. God was just carrying me along. He had other ideas for me. You have to learn sometimes that even when you do things right—and I believed we did the right thing—that doesn't mean the outcome is always going to be ideal for you. Sometimes in life, you have to do what's right no matter what. I knew when we delayed the effective date to abolish straight-ticket voting until 2020 it put me at risk, but I still knew it was more important to get the bill passed than to blow it up just because it might hurt me.

As I neared the eastern edge of Louisiana and drove toward Mississippi, my mind began to shift from the past to the future. I could have spent all the time in the world thinking about the past, but, at the end of the day, I couldn't change it. I made the decision that my time was better spent thinking about the future.

When I reached Mississippi, I veered off the freeway onto the back roads. One of the things I've grown to appreciate as I've aged is that my great-aunt put together a book of my family's ancestry. When I decided to head to the mountains, I packed the book. My family came to America in 1626 and settled in Williamsburg, Virginia. My paternal grandmother's line bore the name Travers (changed to Travis before immigrating to America), and, to this day, you can drive by and see their home, the Travis House. My oldest ancestor on record fought with William the Conqueror at the Battle of Hastings in 1066. My family has a long history in this country, but in some ways, I felt we hadn't come very far. Maybe things would have been different had they not been south of the Mason–Dixon line, but that's just where they grew up.

As I weaved through Mississippi I stopped in Laurel, where my dad's side of the family eventually settled. I went past the homesteads and to the cemetery where I stopped at gravesites and looked inside the book to read about my ancestors. *What would these people think about me?* I wondered. *Am I upholding a family legacy that the generations in the future would be proud of?* I remember looking inside the book at one gravesite and reading that one of my ancestors served in the Virginia House of Burgesses and another ancestor fought in the Revolutionary War. Someone in my family has fought in every war since. It made me feel good, but I wondered if I would be someone whom people might read about and be inspired by another one hundred or two hundred years from now. I realized life was bigger than this one moment; it was just one incident in my life. I needed to find a way to get back on solid footing. I prayed and talked to God (sometimes not very pleasantly). Where was I going to go from here? My kids hadn't seen me lose in hardly anything as they were growing up. There isn't anything wrong with being disappointed in a defeat, but I needed to figure out how I was going to present myself to them long term, not just in what I said but in what I did so that they could learn a lesson as well. I wanted to make sure when I went back home to Texas that I had my act together.

It was quiet when I reached the mountains. Most of the summer residents had gone back to Florida. I don't journal every day, but at big moments in my life, I'll write down in a journal what happened, how I'm feeling, and what I'm thinking to help me process it. When I put it down on a piece of paper, it doesn't look as near of a big deal as I made it in my mind and heart. "OK, so you got beat, what the heck?" I still had a healthy family, I was financially secure, and I had served with integrity. As I wrote, I got it all out of me. By putting it down on paper I found, "This snippet of time in life is *not* all of who I am." I was going to be judged by how I reacted and how I responded to this disappointment. I determined that I would probably continue to be disappointed, that time would have to take care of that. But my actions could not relay that disappointment. Even when I didn't feel like it, my actions had to be different.

Sometimes if you do what you know is right (despite how you might feel), your heart will catch up. That's what I wanted to do. If you wait for your heart to catch up, you may have already missed the opportunity to do the right thing. I learned that ego and self-satisfaction are elixirs that beat you, and you don't even know they're overtaking you until you wake up one day and they're not there to beat you anymore. When there's a defeat in your life, you have a decision to make: are you going to focus on the bitterness of the defeat, or are you going to be open for the next blessing? Because if you're not open to the next blessing, it might not be there for you.

The Story of *Artic*

As a stranded pilot named Overgård buckled a sled around his waist and began to pull an injured woman across the snowy landscape of the Arctic Circle in the movie *Arctic*, I couldn't help but relate it to the lessons we learn from the red wagon.

When we first meet Overgård, he's been stranded for two months and is stuck in a daily routine of checking for fish on his makeshift fishing lines and manning a distress beacon. Days after we meet him, a grizzled Overgård shows a rare excitement when his beacon flashes green and he notices an orange rescue helicopter off in the distance. He shoots his flare, and the helicopter pushes through the snowy conditions toward him. As the helicopter struggles through the wind, unsteadily tipping back and forth, Overgård's wide smile turns to horror and then tears. His lifeline falls out of view and crashes into a snowy valley. When Overgård makes his way to the helicopter he finds that only one of the two pilots has survived. He rips off the door, straps the woman pilot to the sheet of metal, and pulls her to his camp. She is badly wounded with a large gash on her side. Overgård's sole mission turns to keeping her alive.

When days pass without anyone coming to rescue them, Overgård pulls out his map of the Arctic Circle and begins plotting a route to a safe refuge that appears to be a two-day trek. He loads the woman on an orange sled, buckles it around his waist, and begins pulling across the snowy terrain.

Although Overgård has plotted the entire route to avoid obstacles, when he gets to the farthest point he's ever reached, he stops and looks aghast at a steep, rocky slope. "It's not on the map!" he says in frustration. He pulls out the map. Another route would add three days to the already dangerous trip. If he can just get the sled up the hill, a flat route lies ahead. So he carries the rope to the top and begins to pull the woman up the snowy incline. He pulls and pulls, but she slides back down. He tries a second time, but with each pull, he loses grip of the rope and she plummets. When he attempts to pull the sled up the hill for the third time, he can't muster the strength. He lies there, exhausted. "We'll take another way," he decides.

Days later, having injured his leg on the longer route, Overgård reaches another hill. He can't pull any longer. He throws everything out of the sled except for the woman and crawls to the top of the hill to explore the other side. When he sees a helicopter landing off in the distance, Overgård slides down the hill and makes a sudden realization. He finally figures out that *pushing* the sled up the hill is easier than pulling. He gets behind the sled, and with all his might he pushes until he reaches the top. While my obstacle wasn't nearly as dire, that's a lesson I needed to learn. We all face varying degrees of obstacles in our life and must ask the question, What's the best way to get over the hill to the other side? Sometimes it's better to pull our wagon, but sometimes it's better to push.

When I lost the 2018 election, I wasn't pulling or pushing. I was stuck. I had to crawl into the wagon and just become cargo. I needed to rest and to think. I needed somebody else to pull my wagon. I needed an Overgård. As a person of faith, I believed God was telling me, "Ron, I'm gonna pull you through what you believe is a dark time. You just sit back there and rest." As I made my way to the Blue Ridge Mountains, I had to climb into the wagon and get the restoration and clarity that I needed so that at some point I could say, "I'm ready to get out of the wagon. Tell me where to push." When we take hold of the handle, we have to have a clear vision. We need to realize when it's best to let go and let someone or something else guide us.

What hurt the most as I reflected in the mountains was the feeling that I had dropped the ball for my family. One of our three children, Daniel, is on the autism spectrum and has battled through difficult moments in his life. During my first House session in 2013, Daniel married a woman who was also on the spectrum. We thought their differences would complement each other—his strengths, her weaknesses, and vice versa. What ended up happening is they compounded each other. We didn't know it. Looking back, I realized I hadn't done a very good job of coaching Daniel on how to be a better husband. Daniel wasn't someone who would self-advocate, nor would he come to me and ask for advice. They divorced in 2016. I don't blame her or Daniel, and I don't know if I could have saved their marriage, but I do think I could have been a better father to Daniel during that time. My biggest regret is that I could have been more present between legislative sessions and campaigns. I put a lot of burden on

Lisa. Daniel's heart was broken, and seizures that began when he was younger started coming back. He was trying to figure out who he was, and the pressure and responsibility of it all fell on Lisa because I was so engaged in the political world. It was painful coming to the realization. Maybe I was being shown that I had been so hyperfocused that I forgot other things—important things.

Some neat things can emerge from disappointment and heartbreak when God takes you back and reminds you of good things that occurred in the midst of the pain. He showed me some of those moments. For example, when I had returned to the statehouse in Austin after my loss, a Democratic senator came over to me and said, "Ron, I miss working with you so much." She didn't have to do that. She didn't owe me anything. That was my reassurance that while I wasn't perfect, I did some things the right way because I believe people saw me as a statesman. I was taught that a righteous heart is not without sin. Even though I wasn't perfect, I found that I had a righteous heart, and the righteous heart has a lot more going on than I knew.

Finding the Next Blessing

After ten days of solitude, I was ready to return to Dallas and do my best to put the loss behind me. Although I certainly still thought about it, I felt better coming back. We enjoyed a nice Christmas as a family, but the moment of truth hit me a few days later when I went out to the garage and had to remove the "elected official" Texas state license plates from my Silverado.

I still had to decide whether I was going to run again so the defeat lingered in my mind. What you learn about politics is it doesn't just end and it's over. I had people asking me all the time, "Are you gonna run again?" I remember sitting down with John C. Maxwell sometime in 2019 and laying out all my options. He looked at me and said, "Why would anybody want to run for public office after that?" I didn't dwell on it, but I did contemplate it actively. We even polled voters and felt that I had a pretty good chance to win. But I also knew things were changing and the Republican Party needed to run fewer fiftysomething white guys. They needed to run more women and more people of color. I decided that the best thing for District 65 was to find a woman to run and help support her campaign. I was ready for whatever was next in my life. I had made my decision.

What I've learned is, if you spend all your time trying to figure out why a door is shut on you, you'll never see the next open door. With any major disappointment in your life or fork-in-the-road moment where something didn't go the way you thought it should or you wanted it to, there is a choice to make. Even though I had lost and didn't enjoy how I felt about the result, as well as missing the opportunity to leave the legislature on my terms, God showed me that he is still in the business of blessing his people. A few weeks after my loss, I received a call from the new Speaker of the House. I had helped lead a big meeting to have roughly forty representatives announce support for him on the very first day he filed for Speaker. Ironically, I didn't get to vote for him. He was upset I had been beaten but said, "Ron, I'm going to be meeting with the Governor in the next week or two. Would you like an appointment?" Maybe this was my blessing. I hadn't thought about it, but I told him I was willing to serve in whatever capacity Texas wanted me to serve. "I've really been interested in transportation," I told him. The way the Texas transportation system works, there are five commissioners for the Texas Department of Transportation (TxDOT), and they're all appointed by the Governor. There was an opening. "I don't think that'll be a problem," he told me. Three days later, he called me back. "The Governor would prefer that you serve on the board of Texas Mutual Insurance Company and replace the outgoing chairman," he said.

In my six years in office, I had never heard of it, but it became my first blessing. In 1991, the state started Texas Mutual as a workers' compensation company when no other insurance companies wanted to write policies in Texas. The Governor appoints five of the nine board members. "If that's what the Governor wants," I said, "I'm happy to help." I went back to Austin to meet with the Governor's chief of staff. Through our discussion I was able to see that Texas Mutual had a lot of similarities to an investment firm: we were responsible for safely managing assets of our policyholders for their benefit when needed—in this case when an on-the-job accident occurred. My experience with Retirement Advisors of America (RAA), the investment firm I helped form in 1991, had put me on the radar. I saw that you don't have to be elected to influence public policy and that how you conduct yourself in one season of your life absolutely has an effect on how people see you in your next season of life. For God to be able to do something in your life doesn't mean you have to be center stage. You can be the person in the background and still have the most influence. Those have been good lessons for me to learn.

My new blessings allowed me not to look back very often at the closed door. It made me look at the door that was open ahead of me because those doors don't stay open forever. A door closes, and if you've been looking back you don't even realize it's closed, and you wonder why nothing else happens. Well, it's because you were looking back. Sometimes in life you have to leave the closed door behind and take the next uncomfortable step.

~ Chapter 2 ~
A.C.T. (Action, Consider, Takeaway)

Action

List a major unexpected disappointment or defeat you have experienced.

Consider

How did you respond? Did your focus on the disappointment cause you to miss a potential blessing?

Takeaway

Don't be afraid to rest and reflect, but don't pity yourself. Prepare *now* as to how you will react to defeat or disappointment. Look for the next blessing!

CHAPTER 3

The Next Uncomfortable Step

*I*t was unfortunate luck that I had lined up against Eddie Malone during two-a-day football practice my junior year of high school. I was a scrawny five-foot-nine, 165-pound kid, and Eddie was anything but. In Junction City, Arkansas, we had pine trees, and when they reached a certain age, millworkers would harvest them and turn them into pulpwood. During the summers, local kids would haul the logs. Eddie was the prototypical athlete and our star running back. He was six-foot-two, 220 pounds and could probably run the 40-yard dash in 4.5 seconds or better. We lined up for the Oklahoma drill, and I guess I wasn't very smart. When I reached the front of the line, Eddie stood across from me.

We stood facing each other between two rubber dummies. Eddie was the running back with the ball and I took my stance across from him as the defender. We'd meet in the middle and see if Eddie could get past me or if I could make the tackle. It was a true David versus Goliath matchup. Eddie had fifty-five pounds on me, not to mention his Southern pulpwood strength. The rest was a blur for me. When the whistle blew, I rushed ahead and made the perfect hit on Eddie, bringing him to the ground. Maybe he wasn't expecting it. Maybe he wasn't going full speed. But as soon as it happened, my coach pulled me off the ground in excitement. "That's my middle linebacker right there!" he shouted. From that day forward, I never sat out a play. There are moments in life where you gain confidence, and I still remember the confidence that coach instilled in me that day. I didn't get it at home. It's not that my parents didn't want me to be successful in athletics; it just wasn't a priority for them.

There was nothing very special about me or my background growing up. In a lot of ways, my life was pretty generic. I was born in Baton Rouge, Louisiana, and grew up as one of four children in a family that moved from city to city across the South. My mom taught kindergarten; my dad was a band director. My grandparents were good people. My dad's father was a train engineer, and my grandmother was a homemaker (and baker of incredible pies!), but they died before I was a teenager. We didn't live close to them so I saw them only occasionally. My mom's father had an eighth-grade education but had become a fairly successful small farmer and home builder in north Louisiana. One of the greatest educations I received was the summer my parents sent me to live with Grandpa and Grandma Martin. Despite their lack of education and their own relatively poor beginnings, they had done pretty well, but they weren't super successful from a financial or public service standpoint. My mom and dad met at a little school called Louisiana College in Alexandria, Louisiana, and married soon after. They didn't come from any financial means, so they put themselves through school. After they got married, my parents moved to Baton Rouge, where my older brother and I were born, and my dad became the music minister (now known as a worship leader in many churches) at Parkview Baptist Church. We moved around quite a bit growing up. My sister, who is two years younger than I, was born in Monroe, Louisiana, before we moved to Homestead, Florida, where my dad was the minister of music at First Baptist Church of Homestead. I remember living through Hurricane Betsy in 1965. I can still see the water rushing under our front door. Not long after, my youngest brother was born in Miami.

For as long as I can remember, we were always short on money. Growing up, we lived on what I called the Oreo Diet. Since both of my parents were primarily schoolteachers, they got paid once at the end of each month. On the first day of each month, we'd pile into the car with mom and go grocery shopping for the entire month, trying to spread the budget far enough to feed six people. Each time we'd get groceries we'd buy a pack of Oreos. I knew when we ran out of Oreos, things were going to be pretty slim for the rest of the month. That's how I judged our financial wherewithal. The last week of the month was always a little light. I don't know why, but it always bothered me that money was such a big part of our life. And yet we didn't have any. Everything we did focused on "What does it cost?" or "We don't have enough for that." It all revolved around money, and it just drove me crazy, even as a little guy.

It hit me especially hard in the summer after the fifth grade. We lived in Rector, Arkansas, a small town in the northeast corner of the state. I was ten years old, and we had finally settled down enough for me to play my first year of Little League baseball. Toward the end of spring, right as school was about to let out, our parents sat us kids down. "This summer, we're going to move to Newport, just for the summer," they told us. "Dad needs to have a job this summer and needs to make money. We're just going to pack up and move there, and we'll move back after the summer." I remember bawling. I was already signed up for the baseball team, but I wasn't going to get to play. I knew right then that it was all about money. We had to move ninety miles away so we could have more money because my parents hadn't managed the money they had. Other teachers weren't doing that. That was a point of demarcation in my life. *This is ridiculous*, I thought. *I'm not going to do this when I grow up*. I was just ten, but I knew I was going to be different. I had no idea what that meant. But I knew that I needed to be independent as fast as I could. I needed to get out from under my parents' umbrella. I felt like I had to create my own identity. My dad was a very talented musician and singer, and my mom could have been a college professor if she'd wanted. From my point of view as a youngster, they just accepted their situation, maybe because that's all they knew to do or maybe there was some other reason. I just knew I didn't enjoy having everything controlled by money—primarily the lack thereof.

Our family ended up settling in Junction City when I was about twelve. It was a town of fewer than a thousand people. Half the town was in Louisiana, and the other half was in Arkansas. It was literally Junction City. Around the same time as our move to the southern Arkansas border, my parents began having marital problems. It was painful for me to find out. My class at Junction City High School had fewer than sixty kids, so I could play pretty much anything. I chose football and baseball, and for a small town, I was above average. Looking back, sports played an important role in my life during high school. They became my escape, my way to get out the hurt and pain from the challenges that my mom and dad were having. During two-a-days, we'd practice in the morning, I'd go work at the grocery store to make money, and then I'd go back for evening practice. It was good for me, but I resented it. There was probably a lot of pent-up anger that came out, and that was a good place for it to come out. After my hit on Eddie, I earned the starting middle linebacker job. I never could have imagined it. I was probably about the size of a cornerback and, while I wasn't slow, I also wasn't superfast.

But I played well above my athletic ability. My first start came against the defending state runner-up, Norphlet. They had reached the one-yard line right before halftime, and a teammate and I joined to make four tackles in a row on the goal line to keep them from scoring. I'll never forget that. It wasn't because I was better. It was only because I believed. The coach instilled that confidence in me. That's what the middle linebacker was supposed to do. I was maybe too dumb not to know I might get myself hurt.

By the time I was fifteen, I was very independent. My mom and dad were continuing to struggle, and in a small town like Junction City, people probably knew it even though nobody ever said anything. I put all my focus into school and sports. I couldn't fix my parents' problems, so I had to pour everything I had into what I could control. I was laser-focused on finishing up and getting out of Junction City so I wouldn't have those burdens hanging over me. My older brother was off at college, and my younger sister and younger brother couldn't escape it because they were still dependent. But I knew I didn't want to live a life of financial mediocrity. I wanted that to stop at my generation. I was determined to take my wagon by the handle, set my own course, and not let someone or something—in my parents' case, money—lead me into my future.

I remember sitting in study hall one day during my junior year when my guidance counselor, Mr. Waller, called me up to the front of the room. His whisper was so quiet. "Ron," he asked, "what are your plans for college?" I didn't really know. Even though my mom and dad couldn't pay for it, I don't think there was any question for any of us kids that we were going to college. But I had no clear vision for the future. "Well," he said, "you've got a very high IQ." I didn't have any idea what that meant, but at the time I guess it meant you were pretty smart. I didn't go around telling people, but that conversation gave me the confidence to know God had given me intelligence that could help me make it in the world in whatever I chose.

One of the things I've tried to teach my kids and anybody I've worked with is to always take the next uncomfortable step. Most people don't grow by leaps and bounds. They do so one deliberate, uncomfortable step at a time. The easiest thing for me to have done when I was lined up against Eddie Malone was to haphazardly do the drill and make sure I didn't hurt myself. I wouldn't have been thought of any less. A lot of people Eddie matched up against got run over. But the uncomfortable thing to do was to give it my all and just see what happened. If I wanted to live a better life, I was going to have to take many uncomfortable steps to get there.

Lessons from the Boys of Pointe du Hoc

When Lieutenant Colonel James E. Rudder was given the assignment for his Second Ranger Battalion, he couldn't believe it. No such mission had ever been accomplished by Army Rangers. Even Lieutenant General Omar N. Bradley, who delivered the assignment, understood its gravity. "No soldier in my command has ever been wished a more difficult task than that which befell the thirty-four-year-old commander of this Ranger force," Bradley would say later. It seemed like an impossible feat.

Rudder had been commanded to ready the Second Ranger Battalion for an assault on Pointe du Hoc, a promontory that juts out into the English Channel and overlooks Omaha Beach in Normandy, France. German forces had fortified the cliff with 155mm machine guns. Sitting atop the one-hundred-foot cliffs, the German army had a clear view of the Normandy beaches and an ability to cover a range of roughly twenty thousand yards with artillery fire. Rudder's Rangers were tasked with destroying the German positions atop the cliff, something the Germans believed impossible.

In the months leading up to the attack on Pointe du Hoc, Rudder formulated a plan and pushed the 250 US Army Rangers from the Second Battalion through rigorous training. They practiced climbing cliffs along the English coast using ropes, ladders, and grapples and marched twenty miles in full gear. But there was nothing that could truly prepare them for the mission that lay ahead.

On the morning of June 4, 1944, the Second Ranger Battalion boarded boats and began the hour-long journey across the choppy English Channel. Cold water rushed into the boats, and fog made it difficult to locate Pointe du Hoc. As they pushed across the sea, one of the boats capsized, leaving twenty-two men behind. As the Rangers arrived on the eastern shores, the Germans began firing their machine guns, killing fifteen soldiers before they could step foot on the narrow Omaha Beach. As the three groups of soldiers began scaling the one-hundred-foot wall using rope and steel ladders, bullets whipped past them. Still, they pressed on. Within ten minutes, the first Rangers had reached the cliff. When the remainder of the soldiers reached the top, they realized the Germans had moved their guns inland and replaced them with wooden decoys made from painted telephone posts. Exhausted and wounded, the Rangers regrouped and headed south, where they located five of the six machine guns 250 yards inland. While the Second Ranger Battalion accomplished its mission on D-Day, it didn't come without cost. Of those who served, 77 were killed, 152 were wounded, and 38 were listed as missing in action.

In 1984, on the fortieth anniversary of the incredible amphibious attack, President Ronald Reagan delivered one of my favorite speeches.

At dawn, on the morning of the 6th of June, 1944, 225 Rangers jumped off the British landing craft and ran to the bottom of these cliffs. Their mission was one of the most difficult and daring of the invasion: to climb these sheer and desolate cliffs and take out the enemy guns. The Allies had been told that some of the mightiest of these guns were here and they would be trained on the beaches to stop the Allied advance.

The Rangers looked up and saw the enemy soldiers—the edge of the cliffs shooting down at them with machine guns and throwing grenades. And the American Rangers began to climb. They shot rope ladders over the face of these cliffs and began to pull themselves up. When one Ranger fell, another would take his place. When one rope was cut, a Ranger would grab another and begin his climb again. They climbed, shot back, and held their footing. Soon, one by one, the Rangers pulled themselves over the top, and in seizing the firm land at the top of these cliffs, they began to seize back the continent of Europe. Two hundred and twenty-five came here. After 2 days of fighting, only 90 could still bear arms.

These are the boys of Pointe du Hoc. These are the men who took the cliffs. These are the champions who helped free a continent. These are the heroes who helped end a war.

When I think about the heroes who scaled Pointe du Hoc on that fateful date, I think about the incredible obstacles those Army Rangers had to overcome and the uncomfortable steps they had to take. When Rudder was given the impossible assignment, he had to create a vision that made it possible. He had to take the handle and guide his boys. And when those brave soldiers learned of the daunting task ahead of them, they had to trust those guiding them, even when they couldn't see over the cliff.

We can learn so much from the Second Ranger Battalion. As they climbed the wet ropes, dodging enemy artillery fire, they couldn't be worried about the direction they were going; they could only be thinking about getting on that rope and climbing. Sometimes in life, you have to keep pushing. Even though there's risk and you don't know what's on the other side, you have to keep going. You have to take the next uncomfortable step.

Taking the Uncomfortable Step

The day I graduated high school at seventeen years old was the last day I lived with my parents. I had decided that I wasn't going to get sucked into their issues. I had to move forward.

My parents had divorced earlier during my senior year of high school. I had a good relationship with my mom, but she was taking my younger brother and sister and moving to Baton Rouge. I knew there wasn't anything there for me. My dad was off doing other things. I had to rid myself of that baggage of mediocrity. I didn't have a plan for what that would be, but I knew I was comfortable enough with myself that I could make it on my own. I was totally independent of my family from a financial standpoint and, honestly, from an emotional standpoint too. I didn't have much money when I graduated high school so a buddy and I rented a small, rundown two-room apartment (if that's what you want to call it) above a garage in El Dorado, Arkansas, about twenty miles north of Junction City. I knew I wanted to go to college. I received a walk-on offer to play football for a small college, but by that time I wasn't interested in playing college football. So I enrolled at the El Dorado branch of a small college, Southern Arkansas University. To pay my bills I worked overnight at the local feed mill, where they made chicken feed. Interestingly, one of the main ingredients of chicken feed was dead chickens—baby chickens that hadn't made it. The plant would process them in large vats, turning them into a powder so they could be pressed into pellets. It was an interesting summer, to say the least.

A few days into my time at Southern Arkansas University, I met Lisa. We had two classes together—biology and psychology. She always tells people we had biology and psychology, and both of them worked! A few months later we started dating. I liked her family. Her dad was a deputy sheriff and her mom worked at the local gas company. Lisa was from El Dorado, which was a town of about twenty-five thousand. In my eyes, she was a city girl. She had four hundred people in her graduating class; I had fifty-seven.

At the end of our first year at SAU, in the spring of 1979, Lisa and I decided we were going to transfer to Louisiana Tech in Ruston. We were working on getting our college loans that summer when I was playing softball on a local team. "Hey, there's a job open where my wife works if you're interested," one of the players told me. By then I had begun working full time delivering groceries for a local grocery store. "What is it?" I asked. "Murphy Oil," he said.

Everybody who lived in El Dorado knew Murphy Oil. It was a Fortune 500 company and the biggest employer in town. Murphy had a program where they'd reimburse two-thirds of your school tuition if you maintained a B average. It seemed like a pretty good deal to me. I went across town and applied. The job was in the mailroom, which was the lowest level you could start in. I was hired soon after and went to work in the mailroom, delivering mail throughout the company and picking it up at the local post office. I worked days and went to school at night. Instead of going to Louisiana Tech, we stayed in El Dorado.

I was nineteen years old, and there was nothing that necessarily pointed toward me carving a new path. Tell me what you think about this guy: He graduates high school, doesn't have any money for college, lives in a garage apartment with a buddy, works overnight at a chicken-feed plant, his mom and dad are out of the picture, and he takes a lowly job in a mailroom. And, by the way, because money is so tight, he moves into his girlfriend's parents' house and they put a bed in an out-of-the-way hallway. That's a true story. It's how my new life began when I took the uncomfortable step of going out on my own. Lisa's mother wasn't quite sure about me, which I understood. The funny thing was, Lisa was talking to her grandmother, who lived just two doors down, and her grandmother said to her, "Don't you give up on that Ron Simmons. He's gonna be president of something someday. You hang on to him." I can tell you, there weren't any signs that Ron Simmons was going to be successful! That's a good story on the wisdom of people. Wisdom is being able to look through the clutter and see value. That's what Lisa's grandmother was able to do that day. Because the clutter for most of us would have said, "Run, run as fast as you can!"

Lisa and I got married in March 1980 during our second year of college when I was still nineteen and she was twenty. A year and a half later, we had our first son, Justin. My red wagon was now fully loaded for a twenty-one-year-old kid! Because of what I had gone through, I was mature for my age. I don't think it could have worked out any differently for me. I moved to the first step of what my vision for success was. I couldn't get mired in people's problems that I couldn't control. And for me, that was my parents and my family. The next step was how I was going to create my vision as a successful adult. That was getting married, finding a job, and having children. That's what I accomplished. That level of independence stayed with me through my entire life because once I met those needs and was comfortable with that, then I was looking forward: What's the next thing I can accomplish? What's my next step?

We have pivotal moments every day in our lives that help determine who we become and what we believe. I don't have any idea why I was always willing to take the next uncomfortable step. But as I look back, I now know how important it is for people to be able to take the next uncomfortable step in whatever it is they're trying to do. Whether it's in a relationship, business, or anything else in life, take the next uncomfortable step and see what happens.

~ Chapter 3 ~
A.C.T. (Action, Consider, Takeaway)

Action

Write down the major points of inflection (change, demarcation, pivotal points) in your life to date.

Consider

Did fear stop you from taking one path versus the other in any of these situations?

Takeaway

As you approach the next inflection point in your life's journey (and you will!), commit to taking the next uncomfortable step and not letting fear stop you.

CHAPTER 4

Continue Looking Forward

I was at rock bottom, professionally speaking, when I stepped foot inside the mailroom at Murphy Oil. Each morning I'd pick up the company's mail at the El Dorado post office and deliver it to the offices around the building. At night I split my time between playing softball in the adult league and taking classes at Southern Arkansas University. I wasn't content, but I wasn't discouraged. I saw my stop in the mailroom as my temporary, but important, next uncomfortable step.

My daily routine in the mailroom was monotonous, but there was one important task that always had me looking forward. On a wall in the mailroom was a brown cork bulletin board where all the company notices were posted with pins. Whenever a new job came open at Murphy Oil, someone would stick a piece of paper with the job posting to the board. Being in the mailroom, every job that was posted on the board offered more money than I made, so I put my name in the hat for pretty much any new job. My number one goal was figuring out how I could keep improving myself financially. How could I continue climbing the ladder? Some jobs required a college degree. I couldn't go apply to be a petroleum engineer. But there were many jobs where you didn't need a degree, and I applied for most of them. After putting in a number of job applications, I ended up interviewing in human resources to be a benefits analyst. The job description said I'd help out with things like the company's medical and retirement plans. The job probably should have required a college degree because you needed to understand investments and retirement plans. Back then they called them thrift plans, and they were straightforward. I didn't know anything about human resources but I thought, *What the heck?* I was probably making $600 a month in the mailroom. If the job paid $1,500, it was a big step up for me. It would be a move out of the mailroom, so I was excited about the opportunity.

I had been at Murphy Oil for more than a year when I walked into the office for my first interview with the guy who was going to be my supervisor. Then I interviewed with his boss and the boss's boss and ended up getting the job. After I got the job, my boss's boss, Richard Lewis, called me in one day. "Do you know the reason you got this job?" he asked me. "No, Richard, I don't," I said. He told me the only reason he hired me was that Ben Smith, who was the vice president of administration, had given him a directive: "Do not make your decision without talking to Ron Simmons," Richard had been told. "Well, I don't even know Mr. Smith," I told Richard. I'd been in the mailroom for a while, so I was sure I had delivered mail to his office, but I couldn't remember ever talking to him. "No," Richard said, "it was related to softball." I suddenly remembered my first days in the Murphy Oil mailroom.

I had heard about the mailroom job by happenstance on the softball field. Slow-pitch softball was a big deal in small towns where there wasn't much else to do. All the teams usually had a sponsor to buy the team's uniforms and pay league fees. After I started in the mailroom, I met other people who played softball and wondered, *Why don't we sponsor our own team?* I wanted to see if Murphy Oil would sponsor a team. I put together a one-page proposal, typed it up, and started asking around. I eventually learned that the decision-maker was Ben Smith, who oversaw human resources and administration, including the mailroom. I prepared the letter asking Mr. Smith if Murphy Oil would spend $1,000 to sponsor a men's softball team. Here I was, the lowest person on the organizational chart, and I got an appointment with him. I was nervous when I walked into Mr. Smith's office. I was twenty and he was probably forty-five and reminded me of my grandfather. We sat down and I walked him through my plan. A few days later, his secretary told me that Mr. Smith had decided Murphy Oil would sponsor the softball team. I never thought much of the meeting after that until Richard reminded me. I don't know what it was, but something about that meeting impressed Mr. Smith enough that, when I applied for the job in his department a year later, he told Richard not to decide without talking to me first. Richard, wanting to please his boss, probably decided, "OK, I'm going to hire that guy."

The impact of that little softball meeting taught me a valuable lesson early in life: you never know when you're making a good or bad impression that will stick with someone. That meeting could have gone the other way. I could have totally screwed it up and Ben Smith would have told Richard, "No matter what you do, *don't* hire Ron Simmons." That benefits analyst job got me involved in finance and retirement planning and set me on the trajectory that led me to own a significant share of my own company with $3 billion under management. You never, ever know. The impression you're making is important. I didn't know at the time that I was leaving a trail. But after I got the job and Richard called me into his office, I thought, *Man, that's an important thing to remember.*

As a person of faith, I believe a lot of these moments are the Lord looking at us and tapping us on the shoulder. My move out of the mailroom was all about the next uncomfortable step, whether that was going to Ben Smith to ask for $1,000 as a twenty-year-old mailroom employee or applying for job after job that I probably had no business applying for. That's what I want you to know. Getting a better job, improving your financial situation, or having better relationships is not about going from one spot all the way to the top. It's about how you can get from where you are today to the next step. Take that next uncomfortable step and ask that next uncomfortable question, whatever it is. Sometimes it is to pull the wagon, sometimes to push, and sometimes to go along for the ride.

Prepare for the Unknown

Three days after I was hired to be a benefits analyst in human resources, Richard fired my boss. It had nothing to do with me, but before I could even get to know him, he was gone. The first lesson in what I considered my first real-world job was abrupt. Don't think that just because you're going into something means it will be what it's purported to be. You can't let the unknown freak you out. You have to be flexible.

Had everything gone according to plan, I probably would have been put in my office to do analyst work. John would have been between me and Richard, and I would have gone about my job. Now, there was nobody between Richard and me. I wasn't promoted, but back then affirmative action was a big deal. If you wanted to bid on offshore oil leases, you had to have an affirmative action program and take time in job searches to show you were looking for minority and female candidates. As the search for a replacement went on, I had to step up. I was twenty at the time and Richard was probably thirty-five. Looking back, he was a relatively young guy for his position as head of personnel, but he seemed a lot older than me. Richard and I hit it off. What the sudden change did was give me more exposure to a higher level in the company. Around that time, in 1974, the government passed the Employment Retirement Income Security Act, or ERISA, and companies had a few years to get in compliance. Murphy Oil was in the process of finalizing its compliance with a load of documentation. With the company down a man, I was thrown into the middle of it. I didn't know anything about ERISA or employee benefits. Only a few months before I had been in the mailroom. I faced a critical question: *Are you ready for the next unknown situation?* That may seem like an oxymoron, but that's the question I faced—and one so many people face all the time. The way to be ready for the next unknown situation is to never appear that it's surprising to you or scaring you to the people who matter. I could go home and maybe cry on Lisa's shoulder at night, but I couldn't show emotion to Richard. I had to be ready for whatever I was asked to do. I had to have an open, learning, and accepting mind.

There I was at twenty years old, with no boss, trying to help what was supposed to be my boss's boss make sure Murphy Oil was compliant with our defined-benefit plan. Not long after I started working with Richard, he asked me to fly to Dallas with him to meet with the company's actuaries. I don't even know if I knew at the time what an actuary was! I remember going home and telling Lisa, who had never been on an airplane, "I'm going to Dallas with Richard Lewis, and we're going to go talk to our consulting actuaries." It was so far outside of our realm. I hadn't taken ten commercial flights in my life, and now I was boarding a private Cessna jet with the Murphy Oil emblem on the tail of the eight-seat plane. They had their own pilots, and when we boarded the plane at South Arkansas Regional Airport, they had the newspaper and doughnuts waiting for us. It was pretty stunning for a boy from small-town Arkansas. This was truly a moment to climb inside the wagon, be the cargo, and learn while I rode.

On the way to Dallas, Richard briefed me on the meeting. When we arrived at A. S. Hanson Inc. to meet with the actuaries, I remember walking into a room that had the largest conference table I had ever seen in my life. Richard and I sat down with our actuary and a few other people from the firm. I was young and inexperienced, and I probably should have been quieter, but I remember interjecting questions and ideas. I'd gone through the document myself and made edits. It was almost surreal. As I was talking to them, in part of my brain I was thinking, *I can't believe you're doing this.* I don't remember what happened on the way back to El Dorado, but I knew that in Richard's eyes I was someone he thought had potential. He was open about that, and he started giving me more responsibility when we returned.

Richard hired Susie Foster as an accountant and my supervisor not long after our trip to Dallas. She didn't necessarily know any more than I did about employee benefits, but we got along fine and our families remain friends to this day. Even after hiring Suzy as my supervisor, Richard never stopped engaging with me. He was a father figure. My dad was pretty much out of my life during that period, it was early in our marriage, and our second child was on the way when Richard took me under his wing. It wasn't always easy. Lisa and I didn't have any money back then. I had three cheap suits that I bought at a discount store, and with the way the rotation worked, I had to wear two of them twice a week. One of them was a light tan suit from my junior and senior high school proms. I remember Richard would sometimes comment on my lack of professional attire. Maybe my shoes weren't as polished as they should be, or my suit was the same one I had worn only a few days earlier. I was a little embarrassed because sometimes Richard told me in front of other team members. But it made Lisa *really* mad. She didn't like Richard picking on me. As a mentor, he probably could have delivered the message in a better way, but Richard was essentially telling me what I needed to hear. If he didn't tell me, who was going to? Lisa wasn't going to tell me because she cared for me too much. It never hurt me because I knew that Richard meant well. To me, it showed he cared and I needed to do something about it. I did what I could.

The time with Richard gave me a great opportunity to be introduced to something well beyond what I should have been exposed to. That can happen to a lot of people in life, and you have to be ready for it. While you can't anticipate those moments, you have to prepare yourself. I never could have imagined my boss being fired three days after I was hired, but I was always looking for ways to improve myself and my station in life. I feel like I was more ready than most people for that moment. I didn't go into the benefits analyst job to be a benefits analyst. I went in seeing it as my next step. I didn't have any preconceived notions; I was just able to become an expert at a young age on retirement planning and retirement benefits. I wouldn't have had the opportunity had I not been there, ready for the moment. My friend Dr. O. S. Hawkins says, "God calls particular people to a particular place for a particular purpose." I believe that's what happened. For whatever reason, God placed me in that particular spot at that particular time for the purpose of my being able to carve out an expertise.

Sometimes you don't know when opportunities are going to come. You can't sit and prepare for them. What allowed me to be ready, even at a young age, is I knew my last name wasn't Murphy. My mom and dad weren't wealthy, and I didn't have anything to fall back on—I had no Plan B. Knowing that innately required me to be a sponge, to latch on to anything that was out there in front of me that

I felt was an opportunity. My only view was forward. I was not looking back. I didn't have a safety net. Not because my parents wouldn't have wanted to do it; they just didn't have it. So I had to continue looking forward. If you spend part of your time looking back, you might miss something that passes in front of your eyes. I always had to be looking forward, and if something out there was forward, I was ready for it. I believe the Lord blessed me with enough intelligence to be able to grasp what I was able to in my time as a benefits analyst with Richard. If God had placed me in the middle of a drama class, I don't know that I would have been very good at it. When the moment comes for you, will you be looking forward? Are you prepared for the next unknown situation?

Know What You're Worth

During my third year at Murphy Oil, we conducted a massive compensation survey. We wanted to see how our compensation structure compared to our competitors, other midsized to large oil companies we were competing with for employees. We worked with an outside firm on a huge study looking at every single job in the company, showing the average salary for each position.

Murphy Oil was probably having trouble getting quality people to move to El Dorado, Arkansas. Even though the cost of living was less, it wasn't very attractive. The study came back and said, "The average petroleum engineer with ten years of service is making (approximately) $50,000 a year, and you're paying yours $40,000 [this was 1983]. If you want to be in the top quartile, you've got to make these adjustments." It cost the company a lot of money, but they made salary adjustments to be competitive When Richard and Suzy sat down with me, they told me the study had revealed that I was more than 50 percent underpaid. I was making $21,000 and should have been making $30,000 (roughly $100,000 in 2022 dollars).

"We know you're underpaid," Richard told me, "but we can't give it all to you at one time. You wouldn't know how to handle that." I'll never forget that. There was probably a limit on the pay raises Murphy Oil was going to give people at one time, but his comment irritated me. They gave me part of the raise and told me they were going to give me the rest of it later. That got me thinking: *I'm not doing this for the rest of my life.* My last name wasn't Murphy. I didn't want to make any more than I was supposed to, but I wanted to make every dime I was worth. I didn't want anybody saying, "You're working, but we can't pay it to you." I wasn't going to do it. They probably thought, *Here's a guy who hasn't finished his degree and probably has nowhere else to go. We want to keep him and he's going to be valuable, but we can ease into this.* And so I began looking for another job.

I was twenty-four years old and three years into college at Southern Arkansas University with probably another year to go, which really meant another two or three years based on the pace I could go while working full time. I wanted an opportunity where my talent and effort weren't judged on my last name or my perceived situation. I knew a lady who had worked with me in employee benefits at Murphy Oil. She and her husband had moved to Dallas. I reached out to her. "Hey, if you see anything over there, please let me know," I told her. She sent me some options from the *Dallas Morning News.* One was to be the head of employee benefits at Parkland, the big local county hospital famous for its role when President John F. Kennedy was assassinated. It was going to more than double my pay to $51,000. We drove to Dallas for the interview. I could have done the job, no question about it, but they hired someone else.

I applied for another job at North Dallas Bank and Trust, interviewed with them, and they offered me the job to head up the employee benefits area of their trust department. They offered me $30,000, which was still quite a bit more than I was making. I didn't factor in the cost of living, but I knew it was a good opportunity.

Once I got there, there was no limit to where I could go. I went back to El Dorado and told Richard about the job offer. "I'm gonna take it," I told him. Richard was angry and devastated. He felt like he had put a lot into me and that I needed to be patient with him. "Don't be hasty," he said. Lisa was eight months pregnant with our second child and was very nervous. She didn't want to move to Dallas, but I felt it was the right thing to do.

Richard came back to me a couple of days later. "Well, what if we raise your pay to equal what they have?" he asked. "Richard, I appreciate that," I told him, "but if I'm worth that much today, why wasn't I worth that much yesterday?" He didn't have an answer. I went home and told Lisa. It made us more nervous. If I had been making that money in El Dorado, we wouldn't have even looked around in the first place. I went back to North Dallas Bank and Trust. "Look, they've offered me the same amount just to stay," I said. They upped their offer to $35,000. When I told Richard, he asked if I would stay if Murphy Oil would match the salary. "Richard, I just won't," I said. "I just think it's time. I'll never feel right about it."

I had worked in that role with Richard for four years. It was a large chunk of my life, and I was very grateful for what I had learned at such a young age. I went from hourly jobs to the mailroom to starting my corporate career. It wasn't a comfortable decision. I was twenty-four, would soon have two boys, had no college degree, and was leaving a decent job at a Fortune 500 company where they had asked me to stay for a better salary. But I had to look forward.

Later, people would ask Lisa what made her believe moving to a new job in a new city with a young family was going to work. I heard her say one time, "I didn't believe it at all, but I believed in Ron and that's all that mattered." The pressure was on. *Don't screw it up, buddy!*

The whole idea of me talking to Mr. Smith about the softball sponsorship, him mentioning me to my boss's boss, my supervisor getting fired, Richard taking months to hire his replacement, and it all being in the middle of when ERISA was just coming on board is enough for me to believe in a higher purpose. They say everything in life is timing. I agree timing has a lot to do with things that happen. But you'd better be ready for your timing too. A lot of people get put in the right spot at the right time and still don't make the right choice. When I left Murphy Oil, I didn't have a vision for creating my own business or becoming a CEO. I simply wanted to have my hand on the handle of my red wagon and to be in charge of leading it forward. When you're willing to move forward and face the unknown, you can't help but look for what's ahead.

~ *Chapter 4* ~
A.C.T. (Action, Consider, Takeaway)

Action

Spend a couple of minutes writing down your strengths as a person.

Consider

Do you let a challenging situation define who you are, or do you define the situation through your strengths?

Takeaway

Know who you are and what your strengths are so that you can move "through" situations and not just "to" situations.

CHAPTER 5

Finding Your Place on the Team

$\mathcal{W}$e all have an important decision to make in life. Do we want to be great? Or do we want to achieve great things? In our lives, we often face the conflict between those two options.

Softball had a lot to do with Lisa and me being where we were when we moved to Dallas in 1984. It was on a softball field when I first heard about Murphy Oil, and it was because of my passion for the sport that I had left an impression on Ben Smith. Even when we moved from El Dorado, softball was still an important part of our lives. I wasn't a great player, but I was above average. As I got older, I had a decision to make. I could be an above-average player and the star on a mediocre team. Or I could be an average player and contributing member on a very good team. I was always more interested in being on a very good team, whether that was in sports or in business. I've always been more keen on achieving great things as part of a team than being great individually. There are way too many people in this world who want to be the star on a bad team so they can have their name in the headlines. I believe you have to make that decision. Where do you fit on the team? Can you be honest with yourself to understand where you truly fit best? Where do you fit on the red wagon? Sometimes you accomplish more when you are the rear wheels, following a leader, but playing an important role.

Jesus teaches us an important lesson, as recorded in John 6:1–13 when, with the help of his disciples, he feeds five thousand hungry men.

> Jesus crossed to the far shore of the Sea of Galilee. . . and a great crowd of people followed him because they saw the signs he had performed by healing the sick. Then Jesus went up on a mountainside and sat down with his disciples. The Jewish Passover Festival was near.
>
> When Jesus looked up and saw a great crowd coming toward him, he said to Philip, "Where shall we buy bread for these people to eat?" He asked this only to test him, for he already had in mind what he was going to do. Philip answered him, "It would take more than half a year's wages to buy enough bread for each one to have a bite!"
>
> Another of his disciples, Andrew, Simon Peter's brother, spoke up, "Here is a boy with five small barley loaves and two small fish, but how far will they go among so many?" Jesus said, "Have the people sit down." There was plenty of grass in that place, and they sat down [about five thousand men were there]. Jesus then took the loaves, gave thanks, and distributed to those who were seated as much as they wanted. He did the same with the fish.

When they had all had enough to eat, he said to his disciples, "Gather the pieces that are left over. Let nothing be wasted." So they gathered them and filled twelve baskets with the pieces of the five barley loaves left over by those who had eaten.

In this story, we learned that even Jesus didn't work alone—even though he could have. Jesus gave us the example that we can achieve great things with the help of others focused on the same cause. Jesus produced, and his disciples delivered. To achieve great things, sacrifice by the entire crew is important. Everybody needs to believe in the cause and be committed to you, your team, or your company. There are worse things in life than changing team members—such as failing in the cause itself.

One of my biggest struggles at the end of high school was that I didn't get to complete my competitive sports career on my terms. I tore my ACL in the homecoming football game of my senior year at Junction City High School. We had a really good baseball program and won the state championship my junior year. I was able to play third base some by spring of my senior year, and we lost just two games, but I didn't get to go out how I wanted. When you can finish something on your terms, it's much easier to move on—something I found out later in politics too.

Although I couldn't finish my athletic career on my terms, that competitive drive was still very much in me. In El Dorado, after you graduate from high school, playing church-league basketball or slow-pitch softball was just something you did. There wasn't a lot going on. I joined a team. Eventually, I started putting together my own team and was manager. Over time, we built a team called South Arkansas Softball. After five years or so, we were probably the best team in southern Arkansas. We traveled around and played in a tournament somewhere almost every weekend, sometimes playing until 3 a.m. As the manager of the South Arkansas Softball team, I played a lot less than I'd ever played before. If I could find somebody better than me who could play in a game, I would let that person play. We had only twelve players so everybody got to play plenty, but sitting on the bench didn't bother me. I would rather the team win every single time than for me to have even one at-bat.

Many valuable life lessons came out of softball. I remember playing in a tournament in Jacksonville, Arkansas, near Little Rock Air Force Base. We were matched up against Bale Chevrolet, a team out of Little Rock that was always one of the best teams in the state. Their guys all looked like monsters. In the first inning, they scored ten runs. After they hit, our third baseman, Bill Foster, yelled to the group, "Don't worry about it. We get to hit too!" We came back and beat them. It was an important lesson. Even when it may look like you're down, you still have an opportunity. *Boys, we get to hit too.* Too often we forget that really all we need in life, and all we can hope for, is a chance. If you've defeated yourself before the opportunity plays out, then why did you play the game in the first place?

We were playing one hundred games a summer, and luckily Lisa is an easygoing person. I think she probably went back to her grandmother's statement, "You know what, that guy can be president of something." I don't think Lisa liked the long hours I worked or the time I was away on weekends. It probably hurt her, and I wasn't as sensitive as I should have been. While I worked, she mostly stayed home with the kids, so she was all by herself. When we moved to Dallas, we didn't know one soul.

As the kids got older, I became more interested in watching them play than traveling to play softball myself. But there was one valuable lesson I learned during a trip to Houston for a regional tournament. It was a double-elimination tournament, so if your team lost its first game it was still alive—you just had to play a lot of games to get to the championship. Somewhere along the line we lost, so we were playing a lot of back-to-back games. We had only eleven players, meaning we had one extra player because you always had ten players on the field in softball. As the tournament wore on, everybody was tired and sore. We reached the semifinal game and one of our better players, Pete, who had played major college football, asked out of the game. "I just don't want to play, my ankle hurts," he said. He came out of the game, and everybody was pretty upset. Pete was our center fielder and fastest player. We shuffled around the lineup, and I had to go in and play.

To this day, I don't even remember if we won or lost, but I remember the moment as a story that I would tell my kids. We called it the "Pete Syndrome." It means that you don't quit. You don't give up on other people if you can possibly avoid it. That's not something you do in life. As a teammate, a coworker in a relationship, whatever it might be in life, you don't want to be Pete. We still laugh about it and use it to this day. Thankfully, Lisa didn't "Pete" me!

A Knock on the Door

I always said if I ever lived in Dallas, I was going to attend First Baptist Church of Dallas. I grew up a Baptist and had Baptist preachers scattered throughout my family going back three hundred years. Rightly or wrongly, we were indoctrinated. I had heard all about First Baptist Dallas and Dr. W. A. Criswell. They even had a bowling alley in their church!

I was still driving back and forth from Dallas to southern Arkansas playing softball with my buddies that first spring. One Sunday morning while I was away, Lisa heard a knock on the door. *Who the heck could that be?* she wondered. We didn't know anybody. It turned out to be two older ladies who went on visits on Sunday mornings because they knew people at home weren't at church.

"Hey, we'd love for you to come to church," they told Lisa. Oddly enough, they were from First Baptist Dallas. We attended First Baptist for the first time on Easter Sunday in 1985. We fell in love quickly. The next night, some people from church visited us: Wade and Melissa Allen and Karol Ladd (her husband, Curt, who is now a thirty-five-year friend, couldn't make it that night). We talked, and they invited us to Sunday School class the next week. I didn't know it at the time, but the way First Baptist Dallas kept the church feeling small was by putting fifteen or so couples together in a Sunday School class. Even though you knew you were part of a big church, you were part of a smaller group. There were dozens of different classes, each one with couples grouped by age. Nobody knew who we were. We were from Arkansas, so they probably looked at us a little funny. But we were all at about the same stage in life. We had new kids and were just getting started in our careers. The relationships we built in that Sunday School were lifelong. The insurance agent, lawyer, and CPA whom I still use today—plus three longtime business partners—are people I met as a result of attending that class. After church, we'd go out for lunch together with all our young children and, man, when we left, it looked like a tornado had hit the poor restaurant with crackers scattered everywhere on the floor. The experience gave me some guy friends and gave Lisa some girlfriends. We felt like we belonged to something together. We were part of a crew.

I had told Lisa if we ever changed churches, I wanted to meet the pastor. "I'm not going to just go down there without meeting the pastor," I told her. "Dr. Criswell doesn't want to meet with us," I remember her telling me when we got to Dallas. When we decided we were going to join First Baptist Dallas a few weeks after our Easter Sunday visit, I called the church. I reached the secretary and told her we were interested in joining and would like to meet the pastor. "Sure," she said. "Come on over!"

When we arrived, we walked into this long, narrow, ornate-looking office filled with antiques. It was dark and dimly lit by lamps. "Hello, lad," Dr. Criswell said in a deep Southern accent. It was like he literally had the voice of God. You would have thought there was nobody else in the world, the way he talked to us and loved on us that day. That experience reiterated another valuable lesson, one I had learned not long before at a softball tournament in Arkansas. In slow-pitch, there was always back-and-forth about replacing the softball. As the game wore on, the ball would get softer with each hit. You always wanted to play with a new ball if you could, but the umpires were sensitive about changing the ball out unless it was hit out of the park. During a tight game, with one of our home-run hitters coming up, I told the dugout, "I'm gonna see if I can get a new ball put in there." Their eyes rolled back in their heads. "They're not gonna let you do that," they told me. But I walked past the umpire and casually made my pitch. "Hey, how about a new ball?" I said. Without hesitation, the umpire put a new ball in play. The other team was stunned. You never know until you ask! There are times when you are the only one to take the wagon by the handle and lead. This often happens with your family—don't be afraid to take that handle and pull that precious cargo.

The knock at our front door and the call to visit First Baptist Church and Dr. Criswell couldn't have come at a better moment in our lives. When I took the job at North Dallas Bank and Trust, Lisa stayed in El Dorado. While she was there, her grandmother passed away. She was elderly, but you're never really ready for it. About a month after Lisa moved to Dallas, we got another call. Her mother, who was just forty-two, was in the hospital in a coma. She had been having headaches for about a week, and the doctor couldn't figure it out. We found out later she had an aneurysm at the base of her brain. Here we were in Dallas with a toddler and a baby, Lisa had just lost her grandmother, and now her mom was brain-dead. The family moved her down to a better-equipped hospital in Shreveport, Louisiana, but it was too late. The family ended up having to take her off all life-support systems. It was difficult for us but, oddly, it was a blessing that we had moved. When we returned to Dallas from the funeral, even though in our hearts we were sad, there weren't constant reminders around Lisa to keep her in grief.

We loved First Baptist. Back then we'd get up and go to church on Sunday mornings and then go back Sunday nights. On Wednesday nights, I'd meet Lisa there after work and for two dollars we'd have a nice chicken-fried steak or spaghetti dinner. The kids would head off to choir practice or class and we'd sit around with our friends talking about sports and life. The best takeaway from Dr. Criswell was practical. He'd always say, "I've never seen a little child come to church by themselves." If you wanted to get young moms and dads like us in church, you had to have the nicest facility. You could be really high up spiritually, but you had to get people to come. You had to put together a team focused on one common cause.

Building a Volunteer Army

The closest bonds in life are always made when people have volunteered to participate. There's an old saying: "You can choose your friends, but not your family." One of the good things about any sports team or group you're a part of is the commitment. Nothing is better than a volunteer army.

When someone joined Southern Arkansas Softball, nothing else mattered. It was an integrated team with southern Arkansas rednecks and African Americans from all walks of life, with different backgrounds, working in a variety of vocations. We had lawyers, oil-field roughnecks, and teachers. Every other team was similar to us. They had voluntarily come together to participate. For us, it was a little bit more than just Tuesday night softball and pizza and beer afterward.

It was competitive, and we expected our teammates to take it with the same level of energy and enthusiasm. But the reason you felt such a sense of accomplishment when something good happened, or even disappointment when something didn't go well, was because you knew that everybody had chosen to be there for a common cause. They weren't conscripted to be there; they weren't there by birth. They had chosen to be part of the team. The bonds we formed through everybody making the same decision to be a part of the same team were strong. We loved on one another and got to know one another's wives and kids. Nothing else mattered. Nobody cared one bit about someone else's politics or beliefs. As we are reminded in 1 John 1:7, *we are all the same blood.*

I realized later in life that politics wasn't so different. When I was elected to the Texas House of Representatives, I looked around the House floor of the Texas state capitol that had been standing there in that same spot, with those same desks, for almost 150 years. As I looked around on that day, I realized that even though I had many differences with many of the people on that House floor, the only people in the world who knew what it was like to be there—what it took to get there and the responsibility that came with it—were those people inside that little brass railing at the time. We all chose to do it.

When it comes to softball or anything else that you join in life, what you choose to join and stick with and are successful at often have a greater impact on you than something that was forced on you, without the option to join. The beauty of our softball team was the idea that we selected one another. In so many other aspects of life, you don't get to make those choices; somebody makes them for you. When you choose to be a part of something with other people who are choosing to be a part of the same thing, it allows you to achieve great things. Choose to be a part of something, surround yourself with good teammates, and work hard to achieve common goals. Any team you're on—whether it's a marriage, family, work, sports, politics, or church—is all about joining by choice and deciding where everyone fits on the team wagon. When you figure this out, the whole is certainly greater than the sum of the individual parts.

~ *Chapter 5* ~
A.C.T. (Action, Consider, Takeaway)

Action

List the teams you are on in the various areas of your life and the key team members on each of these teams.

Consider

Are you the only member on some of your teams? If so, it is not a team. Would the team members you list also consider you a key member of their team in that area?

Takeaway

Be purposeful in creating teams in the key areas of your life, and be selective when choosing team members—then stay with them! Longevity builds trust, and trust binds relationships.

CHAPTER 6

The Fear of Failure

*W*hen Captain Augustus "Gus" McCrae emerges through the front door of his old Western home in the opening seconds of the 1980s miniseries *Lonesome Dove*, he sees two of his pigs fighting over a rattlesnake and shouts to scatter them from the front porch.

"Go on, get out of here!" he yells. "Go on!" As Gus sits down on his rickety wooden chair, twists the cap off his jug of whiskey, and takes a swig, you get the sense this is just another day.

Gus and his friend Captain Woodrow Call are former Texas Rangers living in Lonesome Dove, Texas, along the Rio Grande River, where they run the Hat Creek Cattle Company. They are old and retired and have been settled into their listless lives for nearly fifteen years when we meet them. Gus fills his days drinking whiskey, gambling, and chasing women. Woodrow is tough but stoic and longs for the adventure of his days as a Ranger. When friend and former

Ranger Jake Spoon arrives back in the Texas border town after years away, Gus and Woodrow are presented with an opportunity. Jake is on the run from Arkansas, where he accidentally killed a man, and suggests they drive the partners' herd of cattle north through the Great Plains to unsettled territory in Montana. With some hesitance, Gus and Woodrow agree. It's clear the two are looking for a purpose.

"It ain't dying I'm talking about, it's living," Gus proclaims. "I doubt it matters where you die, but it matters where you live." Later, during the group's journey, he adds: "I'd like to see one more place that ain't settled before I get decrepit and have to take up the rocking chair."

To me, *Lonesome Dove* is the greatest miniseries of all time. Many decades after it first aired in 1989, the travails of Gus and Woodrow can still teach us many lessons about life. How many times in your life have you been stuck in place, looking out from your porch with the same déjà vu as Gus? It's easy for us to get so caught up in our work, our financial situation, and the everyday details that clutter our lives that we fall into the same routine and monotonous life. Our wagon gets stuck. We wake up, go to work for eight hours, come home and watch television, go to bed, and do it all over again the next day. We fall into a copy-and-paste lifestyle and don't find the time to get ourselves unstuck. When we stop looking forward and stop taking chances, we end up like Gus and Woodrow, longing to make up for lost time after years of settling into the same routine. When Gus and Woodrow set out for Montana, there is no true reason behind their cattle drive except they both want to find purpose in life and take on the next adventure. Many times in our spiritual, business, and relationship lives, we need to go places we haven't been. But we must be willing to go.

Feeling stuck in life sucks. You may know how it feels. You want to move forward but no matter how hard you try, you just can't. What's even worse is you can see the road ahead but somewhere between your brain and your feet, the signal to move gets lost. It may be that you lack the energy and drive to get going. It may be that outside forces are holding you back. It may simply be that you've been striving for so long under your own power that you've run out of gas in the tank. People with no initiative or vision rarely get unstuck because each day looks pretty much the same as the last and the same as the next. It's hard to get unstuck when you don't have any particular place to be.

The truth is, too many people have no idea where they're going in life so they're unsure when (or if) they'll ever get there. Everybody grows up with a dream, yet so many people settle for mediocrity. They drift when they should drive. They coast when they should cruise. They settle when they should strive. Have you been pulling the handle of your wagon along the same path but are realizing that, as you look around, the view hasn't changed? Is your cargo becoming too heavy to carry? Can you see the finish line to your dream but don't see a clear path to get there? My friend John C. Maxwell once said, "Everything worthwhile in life is uphill." He added, "Going uphill requires intentionality." When you aren't intentional about your life, you're at the mercy of the people and circumstances around you.

As Gus and Woodrow travel toward Montana, the journey is everything they've dreamed of. The destination is worth the journey, even if the friends have to overcome robbers, hostile Indians, and many other obstacles along the way. Gus and Woodrow don't know what's ahead of them when they begin their push north, but they go anyway (and Gus gets one final adventure before—spoiler alert—he dies shortly after they arrive in Montana).

One of the biggest reasons people get stuck in life is the fear of the future. Wondering about the unknown can be paralyzing. You aren't sure what's around the corner, so you keep your head down and keep doing what you've been doing the way you've been doing it. That's why some people stay in the same job for years, mindlessly clocking in and out each day, never looking for a better opportunity. Or why many people settle for a rocky marriage while never doing the work it takes to make it better. When your future is fearful, it's easy to feel stuck because the reality is you aren't moving forward.

I may sound like a broken record, but that's why I've always challenged the people I've mentored to take the next uncomfortable step. There's risk involved in that, but it's the only way to get to places you've never been. When Murphy Oil offered me a raise to stay in El Dorado, I had to take a step back and examine my decision. Maybe it was the fear of falling back into my family's history, but I knew I had to keep moving forward to avoid going back. I was twenty-four with no college degree and probably had no business running a large area of the trust department of a good-sized Dallas bank. There wasn't anything special that you would have seen in my background that would make you say, "Ron, I could have told you that you were going to do that." If you looked at the résumés of the people I was meeting, you would see that they were much more accomplished. I was never intimidated by that. I didn't approach the job timidly. I always had confidence that I was as smart as the next guy. Even when I wasn't, I thought I was. As Gus says in *Lonesome Dove*, "Yesterday's gone on down the river and you can't get it back." That was always my thinking. Life is all about pushing ahead. Just keep pushing ahead.

A Willingness to Learn

I've found the opportunity to learn and grow occurs only when you're going into areas that you don't know much about. You don't usually learn and grow when you stay in the same little spot—only when you face uncertainty. I learned a lot in my four years at Murphy Oil, but I still had a lot to learn in my new role as assistant vice president of a good-sized bank and trust company. How was I able to grow so much? It was because my feet were held to the fire.

My boss at North Dallas Bank and Trust was laissez-faire. He was always there if I needed to talk to him, but he was hands-off. So not yet twenty-five years old, I was overseeing $100 million or so under management. North Dallas Bank and Trust wasn't part of a big conglomerate, but, back in 1985, Dallas was growing fast and there was a new group of people with wealth.

The old money people were still around, but they tended to take their business to Republic Bank downtown. Those new people were in their thirties and forties and were beginning to make their marks in real estate and oil. The timing couldn't have been any better. The new money was beginning to arrive at North Dallas Bank and Trust. I started meeting people who were early in their careers and hadn't quite made it but were on their way up. I would call small business clients who had their retirement accounts with the bank or new people whom the bank had a loan relationship with and see if we could establish a trust relationship with them. I was successful at the company, helping build the trust department faster than it had grown in the previous twenty-five years. But as I began to meet people who were entrepreneurs and business owners, it opened my eyes. *What does my future look like?* I wondered. I was making more money than I had ever made in my life, and I probably could have stayed at North Dallas Bank and Trust and climbed the ranks to the top. Most people would have been happy, and I might have been too. But the people I was meeting had started their own companies and seemed firmly in control of their future. I could tell there were people at the bank whom I might not see eye to eye with, and I didn't want to have that hindrance. I wanted to be the person *in* that position, not the person *under* that person. I wanted to be the person who determined whether or not I was going to be successful through my efforts. That began to attract me to the idea of starting something myself. Even as I accomplished more than most twenty-four-year-olds would have accomplished, I was still ready to take on the next challenge—and ready for new opportunities.

While I was largely on my own to learn, there was a fortysomething guy named Brooks Hamilton in the office who was an ERISA lawyer. While Brooks wasn't affiliated with the bank, we shared some clients and he would give us advice. Brooks was an eccentric guy, and he took a liking to me. I was still trying to get my college degree, taking night classes at Dallas Baptist University. Like in a lot of different seasons of my life, Brooks took me under his wing and was a mentor in my business career. He'd take me to cool, out-of-the-way eating places in Dallas once or twice a week, and I felt like I had somebody whom I could talk to about business and seek advice from. Brooks introduced me to a lot of interesting people, including Charlie Leggett. Charlie ran a small actuarial firm so it was a natural connection. I was handling trust accounts at North Dallas Bank and Trust, Charlie might be doing the administration, and Brooks was providing legal guidance. I had been at the bank for ten months when Charlie came to me with a proposition.

"Ron," he said, "a group of us are thinking about setting up our own private trust company." The idea was to start a nonbank trust company that would manage retirement plans for smaller companies that the big banks and big investment houses had totally forgotten about. We'd specialize in $5 million to $10 million retirement plans for small companies we felt were underserved. "Would you be interested in heading up our sales and marketing?" Charlie asked me. I told him I was interested in hearing more. Charlie was working with partners on funding and said they were going to have funding together in two weeks. It became one of those deals where every two weeks the deadline would change. "We're going to have our funding in two more weeks," they'd tell me.

Lisa and I were enjoying our time in Dallas and Justin had just started kindergarten at a local public school. We were happy. I had been at the bank for probably fifteen months when I got a call from Richard Lewis. "Ron, I don't know if you know, but I left Murphy and I'm at Anadarko Petroleum in Houston," he said. "We've been spun off and we have to do all of our own employee benefits for eight hundred employees. I need somebody to come down here and be my employee benefits supervisor." The job was the same one for which Richard had hired Suzy at Murphy Oil. "We're happy where we are, but I loved working with you," I told Richard. "What's the scenario?" The salary increase was more than 60 percent! It was another valuable lesson: don't burn bridges. You don't ever know where it's going to circle back. It was a good opportunity, and Charlie and his group didn't have the money for the new venture. I even told Richard about it. "Richard, there's a new venture that these people have asked me to be a part of, but they don't have the money," I told him. "They could get it together one day and I might decide to go back." Richard was fine with that. It felt like I was pulling Lisa and our family around, but the move seemed like a no-brainer and the next logical step.

Lisa might have been in the wagon crying by this point. She didn't want to go to Dallas, and we'd finally settled in at First Baptist Dallas and met a group of friends. Now she didn't want to move to Houston. She had essentially lived in the same town her entire life before marrying me so moving from El Dorado to Dallas and then to Houston less than two years later was very hard on her. I am sure I was not as sensitive to that as I should have been. But our apprehension dissipated quickly once we arrived in Houston. We found a nice neighborhood, Kingwood, on the north side of the city, and met new friends who were all about the same stage in life as we were. By this point, my sister was out of college and my younger brother was in college, which meant my mom was all alone in Baton Rouge. So in 1986, we asked my mom to live with us and teach in Houston.

It was a blessing. She taught first grade at a local school and helped out with our kids. At Anadarko, Richard treated me with a lot more maturity and became much more of a friend than the mentor he had been at Murphy Oil. It was a good company that treated people well and didn't have a large stockholder whose name was on the door. I was charged with building the company's entire employee benefits program from the ground up, so I'd travel around to the handful of locations in the Southwest and explain the medical, dental, and 401(k) plans we had put together for the employees.

As you could probably guess, ten months into my time at Anadarko I received a call from Charlie and one of his partners, Bill Bret. "Hey, we got our money," they said. "Are you ready to start?" I was stunned. *Oh, my goodness. What are we doing?* I thought. Bill, Charlie, and a few former Morgan Stanley guys had put together the money. The company was actually going to happen. At the time I left Murphy Oil, I was making $21,000. North Dallas Bank and Trust had offered me $35,000 to leave and I was up to $52,000 at Anadarko. I was doing well for my late twenties, especially in the 1980s. These guys were offering me $80,000 (almost $200,000 in 2022 dollars). So guess what we did? We packed up again and headed back to Dallas.

First Southern Trust Company opened for business in October 1987 as a nonbank trust company. Bill was running day-to-day operations and I was head of sales and marketing. We created a multimanager approach where, because of our size, we could connect small companies with the best money managers in the business to administer their pension plans. These small businesses wouldn't have been able to access them on their own, but by partnering with us, we were able to make the connection. The pool of potential clients seemed endless. But timing is important in business. On October 19, 1987, Black Monday hit. The stock market crashed, sending the Dow Jones Industrial Average plummeting 508 points, the largest single-day US stock market drop in history at the time. The market

THE FEAR OF FAILURE   89

had lost 22.6 percent of its value. We didn't have any clients, so we were fortunate not to lose any money. But it was clear: my safety net was gone.

Was I crazy to have left the comfort of Anadarko? I was making more money, but we could go belly-up at any moment. Nobody likes to fail. I don't like to fail any more than you do. But I've never let that keep me from taking the next step or embracing the next opportunity.

Some people focus on the possibility of failure. I focus on, "This is going to feel so good when it's successful." Maybe I focus on that too much sometimes, but that's what drives me. I've never been driven by not wanting to do something because I'm afraid I'm going to fail. Instead, I take the step because I'm afraid if I don't it would be worse.

A Calling to the Sky

We still didn't have any clients at First Southern Trust when, through a connection, we secured a meeting at the American Airlines head-quarters in Dallas. A year prior, the airline giant had spun off the area of the company that handled all its investments into a subsidiary, AMR Investment Services.

The whole idea was that American Airlines would have its same money managers put together mutual funds and manage the compa-ny's pension plans. But because of the size of their mutual funds holdings, AMR would be able to attract some of the very best money managers in the world. A high-level money manager might not want to come to First Southern Trust to manage $10 million, but they'd certainly be interested in managing $10 *billion* at AMR. The way the mutual funds work, we could piggyback onto their size and gain access to those top-quality money managers and investment experts we couldn't normally access. If we were able to partner with

AMR, we could ally our clients with top-notch financial advisors. I walked into the big conference room confident and determined to simply be myself—a strategy that had worked well before and I was sure would work well again.

When we arrived at American Airlines headquarters, Bill Quinn was waiting for us. Bill was a mid-forties, Irish Catholic guy from Queens, New York, who had worked for American Airlines essentially his entire career. He had been charged with running AMR Investments and was looking for clients as well, so he was eager to hear our business plan. We spent the meeting laying out our plan. We didn't have any clients yet, but if we did, we told Bill, we'd like to use AMR's mutual funds. The entire plan went perfectly. "Sure," Bill said, "we could work with you on that."

At the end of the meeting, as we shook hands, said our goodbyes, and prepared to leave, Bill shouted out, "Hey, wait a minute, you got just another minute?" We turned around and sat back down at the table. Bill explained that they had three or four retired pilots who wanted to use AMR's mutual funds. The problem was, AMR wasn't set up to handle individuals. Bill looked me in the eye and asked if we could help these pilots. "Could y'all set that up? Could y'all handle them? I know it's not your niche, but could you do that as a favor?" We weren't set up for that, either, but we were just getting started and needed all the clients we could get. We'd be the trustee of the pilots' Individual Retirement Accounts (IRAs) and use AMR to invest. It was just three or four. "Sure," I said, "give us the names; we'll be happy to call them." As the head of sales, that task would fall on my shoulders. It turned out to be a godsend.

The next week I made my first phone call to Bob Wilson. I'll never forget him. Bob was a retired American Airlines captain living in Burleson, Texas, a small town southwest of Fort Worth. When a pilot retired at that time, they received their entire retirement in one lump-sum payment. For guys retiring in 1987 who had been with

American Airlines for thirty years, it was probably a $1 million check. They had to put it in an IRA to shelter it from tax, and they'd pull out a little bit each month for living expenses. Many of them needed somebody to invest it. As the old saying goes (somewhat tongue in cheek), "You never invest with a pilot or fly with a doctor because both of them will get you killed." So I called Bob and told him I was with First Southern Trust working with AMR Investments, the people who used to manage his retirement funds before he retired. "Come on out to the house," he told me.

It was a Friday afternoon, and I was getting ready to drive back to Houston to see Lisa and the kids, who hadn't yet moved to Dallas. I was eager to get the meeting over with so I could get on the road. I knocked on the door and a man with a long, white beard opened it. He looked exactly like Santa Claus. Back then, when he was flying, pilots weren't allowed to have facial hair in the cockpit because the planes were a lot more mechanical, and it was deemed a fire hazard. So when pilots like Bob retired, dadgummit, they were going to have a beard! I sat down with Bob at his table and talked through how we could help manage his lump sum. "I just want to stay with the people who helped me make this money so I don't mess it up," Bob said. I had our first client. As I was getting ready to end the meeting and leave, Bob jumped in. "Hey, I got something you might be interested in," he told me. "I don't know if you would be, but just give me a minute." He disappeared into the back room of his house. A few minutes later, he returned with a stack of papers. He handed me a list of 1,500 guys just like him called the Grey Eagles. At that time, pilots had to retire when they turned sixty. This list had names, addresses, and phone numbers of pilots who were fifty or older, many of whom were retired. I had just turned twenty-seven, but by the time I got to my car with Bob's list in hand, I knew exactly what business I was going to be in for the rest of my life. There was no question about it.

I knew I couldn't get all the pilots on the list, but I could get some of them. After the weekend I went back to the office and shared the news with Bill and Charlie. They were excited about that opportunity because we needed to get clients and money in the door. But their vision wasn't focused on retired pilots—it was small company pension plans. That's what they had locked in on because that's the world they lived in. So we started going down dual paths. I still called on people who had small company pension plans, but the pilot side was growing fast, and we had a unique story to tell. We were connected to the people who had helped these pilots make all the money. When they retired, many of the American Airlines pilots would end up where one of the big airline hubs was. At the time, that was Chicago, Dallas, Los Angeles, and New York. If they weren't there, they had probably moved to Arizona or Florida. I began traveling 70 percent of the time to those six locations. Two out of every three weeks I'd spend my time meeting with pilots one-on-one or in a group.

Sometimes when things are really clear to you, they're not clear to others. You have to decide what you're going to do about that. It becomes difficult to move forward toward your goals and dreams when multiple people are trying to take the handle of the wagon and lead the way. As I began adding retired pilots, there was a constant battle at the company. Bill and Charlie didn't really want to be just a pilot business. My argument: until we totally exhausted everything and had every pilot possible, why would we spend our efforts elsewhere? We knew what we were doing in the pilot business, and it was very fraternal. If I went to meet with Bob Smith and said, "Bob, Joe Johnson is a client of ours," he'd say, "Oh, Joe. I was in the military with Joe. If it's good enough for Joe, it's good enough for me." That might not always be the best way to make your decision, but that's how many of the retired pilots made it.

I educated myself on every one of their benefits. What was going to happen to their sick pay? What happened to their unused vacation? What about their flight benefits? What happened to their medical plan? I made myself an expert so I could sit down with Bob and Sue and say, "Let's not talk about your money right now. Let's talk about these things." I spoke their language. We even put together a checklist because, in their decades-long careers, the pilots had become accustomed to going through a checklist before takeoff. Our whole pitch: we were going to know more than anybody else, and if they were happy with the people who helped them make the money, they'd be happy with us.

After a few years, things reached a tipping point with Bill and Charlie. We had raised somewhere near $300 million in assets (the majority of which I had raised), but they were no longer supportive of the pilot effort. They were the ones who had put the money up to start the venture, and they had their vision of managing small company retirement plans. That situation led to another valuable life lesson: every team member has to be on the same path or they can't be on the team. It doesn't mean they're wrong; they just don't fit. At some point you have to have faith in your partners; otherwise, you probably have the wrong partners. I no longer fit on the First Southern Trust team. After years of helping push the wagon forward, it was no longer going the direction I wanted to go. I couldn't keep pushing toward a destination I didn't believe in. I had to build my own wagon. The Morgan Stanley guys from New York were on our side, so a couple of other colleagues and I decided to go off on our own. It was a risky move, but we had a lot of confidence. Even if we didn't get any of the business that was on our books to come with us, it didn't really matter. We knew pilots had to retire at age sixty, and we knew how many people were coming up for retirement each year. It wasn't just American—there was Delta, United, and some of the other big airlines too. We knew we had a model that worked. So we left and set up our own company called Retirement Advisors of America, one of the all-time great name selections, in my opinion.

It was a stable name that wasn't about any one person. There was a bigger vision that would last well beyond any singular person involved with the company.

I was the head of sales and marketing for First Southern at twenty-seven, traveling around the country talking to people who were sixty and telling them, "Trust me to manage your life savings." That's not something *anybody* can do. But it's also something that *everybody* can do because I wasn't anybody special. I want to take your excuses away. You might say, "Obviously *you* can do that. I couldn't do that." That's just not true. You may choose not to do it, and that's fine, but it's not true that you *can't* do it. Helping to build First Southern Trust from zero to nearly $300 million under management and then leaving and starting our own company at age thirty was risky. But that's what you have to decide. Are you strong enough to take the risk in your life?

All of the things I did along the way were risky. I could have been embarrassed. When I went to Dallas to apply for that job at North Dallas Bank and Trust, the guy sitting across from me could have said, "What the heck are you doing here? You're twenty-four years old. You don't have a college degree. Goodbye." All those things could have happened, but I've always been willing to look at the potential value of success being greater than the risk of failure. That has always driven me. I was continually trying to work on ways to get better at what I was doing. That gave me the confidence to take the next uncomfortable step. You have to be willing to take that next uncomfortable step if you want to see what's on the other side. If you don't, that's fine, but you're never going to expand your horizon beyond what you can see right in front of you.

Most people live their life in fear of failure. That's why we find ourselves stuck. Sometimes we can move our wagon forward only when we discover what's been holding us back.

~ *Chapter 6* ~
A.C.T. (Action, Consider, Takeaway)

Action

List the major decisions in your life (so far) and beside each one, write whether you now believe (with the benefit of hindsight) the decision was made out of fear or opportunity. Remember, even when we don't move forward, it is still a decision.

Consider

Think about whether you are more driven by fear of failure or by excitement of new opportunity. Which approach makes you happier? For most of my life, I was driven by a fear of financial mediocrity. While this was a driver, I also realize it caused a lot of stress, mostly self-induced.

Takeaway

Decide what type of motivation is best for you and allows you to be the best you, not just in accomplishing your goals but in being the person you want to be with the people for whom you care the most.

CHAPTER 7

Create Your Opportunity

*W*e hit the ground running with Retirement Advisors of America. The first twenty-six airline pilots I sat down and spoke with said yes and agreed to trust us with their savings to start us down the right path. Clearly, we were on to something big, and our wagon was rolling along smoothly. Then came the proverbial pothole.

It was 1992, and there I sat in a Dallas courtroom looking back at Lisa, who was eight-and-a-half months pregnant with our third child. *What the heck is going to happen if we lose?* I thought. We had laid everything on the line to start RAA, and if we lost the lawsuit, it would all be gone. It was scary to put our fate in the hands of twelve fellow citizens. When it became clear First Southern Trust wasn't interested in the retired pilot business model, I, along with another member of the investment team, Guy, set out to start RAA. It was a small group. Guy and I were joined by Ann, who handled back-office operations, and Maria, who was an administrative assistant. Shortly thereafter, Scott Frost joined us. Scott became a very good friend and would eventually serve as CEO. We knew we had a model that would work, and the three Morgan Stanley backers from First Southern Trust—Jim, Bill, and Rick—put up money to get it started. Everybody owned a little piece. Guy and I didn't put any money up, but we each had a 10 percent stake in the company. When we left First Southern Trust, we didn't take any client lists or call on any of our current clients, although some of them called us and wanted to come over. The way Texas law worked at the time was, even if you had a non-compete, which I didn't, you could take a customer's business if they called you; you just couldn't solicit them. We didn't need to take any customer information with us. The pilot lists were public information, and there were thousands of pilots out there. I learned then, at age thirty, that it doesn't matter whether you're doing it right or not—people can still sue you. First Southern Trust thought we were stealing client information, and RAA's fate was in the hands of a dozen jurors who may or may not have understood the complicated business scenario.

We were fortunate that our investors were paying the legal bills, which ended up totaling $750,000. They could have easily said, "You know what, guys, we're going to cut our losses here." Instead, they fought the battle until the end. I was never concerned about whether I could get a job if the legal battle went sideways, but it was pretty scary. If we hadn't had Jim, Bill, and Rick, RAA would have had to fold because we didn't have the money. They never flinched. I will be forever grateful to those three men. We split our time building up the business and going to the courtroom. Lisa continued to come to the hearings as she reached her due date. Once First Southern completed their side of the case, our attorneys felt that First Southern had not proven their case based on any legal premise. Therefore, we asked the judge to dismiss the case based on First Southern's inability to provide any evidence that would prove we had broken any laws or agreements. The judge agreed with us, and the case was dismissed. Ironically, on the day the judge announced his decision—dismissing the lawsuit and giving us the win—Allie Beth was born.

Once we got past the lawsuit, we were moving and shaking. We were adding anywhere from $50 million to $100 million per year in assets under management. While we started with American Airlines pilots as our lead, we began looking at pilots from other airlines. When we talked to one pilot at American who had flown in the military, there was bound to be a connection. "I flew in the military with ___ and he went with Delta," the pilot would say. "Have you talked to him?" So we would go talk to him too. What was interesting about those pilots was that becoming a pilot was rarely a business decision. For me, going into business had always been a financial decision, not an emotional one. What I saw in these pilots was that flying was an emotional decision— their careers were driven by a sheer love of flying. Many of them would have done it for a lot less money. As I climbed the ladder in business, I thought about my future and building a safety net every day. Those pilots didn't. They thought, *I'm gonna get behind that big wheel, push that throttle forward, and there's nothing better in the world.* They'd be gone for two days and home for three. In their time off they golfed and fished and some even had small farms or other side businesses. It was a pretty golden life. We knew which pilots were reaching the mandated retirement age of sixty and initially tried getting in touch with them about five years before-hand. Most weren't interested then. As the old saying goes, when the student is ready, the teacher appears. Around age fifty-eight, something happened to trigger a willingness for a discussion. The pilots' union would send out information about retirement, and we prepared a checklist of everything they needed to do so that when they reached their sixtieth birthday, everything was in order. At about fifty-eight, pilots were ready to sit down and visit.

We kept our singular focus and within the next few years began making some money, and ownership was happy.

We probably had $200 million under management by 1993, and Guy and I were feeling pretty good about ourselves. We were in Dallas growing the business while Jim, Bill, and Rick kept a close eye on the operations from their bases in New York and Boston. Guy and I were part of the five-person board along with Jim, Bill, and Rick, so they had control of the company, which was only right. As our board meeting neared, Guy and I started having discussions along the lines of, "We're doing all the work, and Jim and Bill and Rick helped us out at first, but they're not the reason this thing is successful. *We're* the reason it's successful." When the three flew into Dallas, we were going to tell them we were tired of making them rich, that we needed more ownership of RAA.

We worked from the thirteenth (ironically) floor of the Occidental Chemical Tower in north Dallas. It was a big, glass office building, and we subleased our space from another company. Jim, Bill, and Rick would fly into town for board meetings and Guy, as president of the company, had a long, narrow, odd-shaped office with a long conference table we'd sit around. When the three arrived, we sat down, began the meeting, and everything was fine. The company wasn't making a profit yet because we were putting everything back into sales and marketing, but with $200 million under management and growing, we were doing well. Guy began our planned message but was stumbling through it. At that time I was vice president of sales and marketing and had a bravado about me. I jumped in and cut Guy off. "Gentlemen, we appreciate you and everything, but we're tired of making you guys rich," I said. "We want to be rich too." Jim, the elder statesman of the group who owned a significant stake in Morgan Stanley stock and was a millionaire many times over on his own, never changed his expression. Bill and Rick didn't even look up. "We're already rich," Jim said flatly. "Next question." We had no response. "Oh, OK," I said. "Well, let's see here. The next item on the agenda is our P&L . . ." We hadn't planned for that response. In addition to being pretty embarrassing, it certainly refocused us on the mission at hand. ·

A Difficult Decision

A year after our brazen demand, in February 1994, I was sitting in my thirteenth-floor office at the Occidental Tower when Jim, Bill, and Rick arrived for our board meeting. Before the meeting, Bill and Rick asked to meet with me privately.

"Ron, in about ten minutes you're going to be the new president and CEO of the company, and Guy is not going to be here anymore," they said. I was stunned. "Jim is meeting with him now. We just can't work with Guy. It's yours if you want it. We'll find somebody else if you don't, but it's not going to be Guy."

I knew there had been conflicts between Guy and ownership because Guy could be obstinate sometimes, but I never expected it to come to that. I was in a difficult scenario. I could have told them I didn't agree with the decision and taken my marbles and gone home, but I weighed the offer and decided the best thing was to stick with it. I wasn't going to go anywhere. I was invested in this thing. Guy wasn't happy with me at all. He called me later that night and cussed me out, saying I had essentially thrown him under the bus, which I hadn't. I had no idea the situation had escalated and reached a boiling point. We've made up since then, but it was a difficult process.

I learned you have to evaluate each situation and determine what's best for you and the people that you care about. And that's what I did. I didn't know I was going to be CEO, but that's what happened. I was thirty-three and I had become CEO of a wealth management company with hundreds of millions of dollars in assets under management. I knew we had the potential to be successful, but I didn't realize we were starting a niche industry. My goal, just like it was when I was seventeen and starting on my own, was simple: *What's the next thing I can accomplish?* The answer seemed obvious to me: make Retirement Advisors of America as big as I could so that I could become financially independent and help the people I care about benefit as well. It wasn't ego-driven. If it had been, I would have named the company Simmons Wealth Management and become the face of the company from the very beginning. I didn't want that. I simply wanted to make sure that my family was taken care of, and I wanted to give other people the same opportunity. Most important, I wanted to direct the attention of what we were building to the firm and the people who made it successful. That way, if I decided I didn't want to be a part of it anymore, it could still survive and succeed without me.

There's a great lesson in that. There are some professions where all you're ever going to do is build an income. Take being a doctor or a lawyer, for example. There's nothing wrong with them, but you have to figure out how to turn some of that income into an asset if you ever want the ability to walk away from the day-to-day of being a doctor or a lawyer. This is one of the great challenges many people have when they start a business. They haven't ever thought this way—and sometimes it's too late. I don't know that I ever actively thought about it when we started RAA in 1990, but I know that lesson to be true in business now: you have to decide whether you want to have an *asset* or an *income*. If you put your name on the door, all you ever have is an income that the name represents. I decided early on that neither my name nor any of our key partners' names were going to be on the door. We were going to have a generic name so that if anybody left or I decided to leave, the company wasn't going to be hindered. We also set up a system where regardless of who brought in the client—and many times that was me—the firm would take care of their day-to-day needs. This gave them value through the company. As the salesperson, Bob might call his new client three times a year and Nancy would check in with them monthly. By the second year, sometimes they didn't even remember who Bob was! We always had two-member teams so there was a backup. I didn't want to have a relationship manager saying, "Hey, I'm leaving and taking all these clients with me if you don't do *x* for me." We had a couple of people try it over the years, but they failed. That was the value of building RAA as an asset. If the company had been so tied to an individual or individuals, its value would not have been that great. Even though key people left RAA over time, we never missed a lick.

Taking over as CEO of RAA in 1994 wasn't optimal timing. Around the same time I was promoted, what today is known as the Great Bond Massacre began. Interest rates shot up, creating an inverted yield curve where short-term interest rates were paying more than long-term interest rates. By September 1994, bond-holders had lost $1 trillion. And yet RAA was surprisingly hitting its stride at the perfect time. Since all pilots had to retire at age sixty (today it's sixty-five), we could generally go back three decades, look at the hiring pattern of airlines, and forecast demand for pension plans. It just so happened that thirty years earlier, in 1964, was the start of the Jet Age. When Pan American Airways sent a Boeing 707 on its first commercial flight from New York City to Paris on October 26, 1958, it ushered in a new era. The Boeing 707 became the most widely used commercial jetliner. During the next decade, passenger numbers quadrupled. Meanwhile, airlines hired pilots as fast as they could find them. A pilot shortage prompted some airlines to hire people out of college and pay for their pilot training. Our business ebbed and flowed based on trends. In the early 1970s, airlines hired almost no new pilots. So thirty years later, in the early 2000s, there were very few pilots retiring. Most of the 1990s, though, was filled with opportunity.

By 1997, we were inching toward half a billion dollars under management, but I was beginning to burn out. My oldest son, Justin, was sixteen and a sophomore in high school, and I could see him slipping away and heading off to college before I could shake my head. I began to wonder, *Is there a way to get out of this day-to-day grind?* I had started in the pilot retirement business in 1987 and had been running full steam ahead ever since. Lisa and I had three kids, including one with special needs, and had built, with the help of a good team, the RAA business from scratch. It took years to break even. I was really getting worn out. I was thirty-six, and I decided to set a goal that I was going to leave the company. I would sell my 10 percent interest and take some time off. I created a screensaver on my computer with six numbers: 12/31/98. On December 31, 1998, I was going to leave.

Dream, Plan, and Make the Effort

To make that goal happen, I put together something I call a Dream, Goal, Plan, and Effort framework. Moving your wagon forward in life takes vision and intentionality. When we get stuck in a rut or find ourselves moving in place, it can be because our cargo contains a lack of knowledge. We don't know what we want, where to go, or how to achieve it; or we lack discipline, meaning we know but don't follow through and do it.

What is your dream? A dream should never be a dollar figure. If I gave you $1 million and stacked $100 bills up in that room with you, you could sit and look at it all day long and it wouldn't do a single thing. Pretty soon, if all it ever does is sit there, it's just combustible material. When people say, "I just want to make a lot of money," it's really not what they want. They want whatever the money provides and can't articulate it. It takes effort to articulate your dreams. From the time I was a kid in southern Arkansas, I dreamed of financial independence. I hated how much money meant to every decision our family made. I never dreamed of a particular salary; I just dreamed of not having to think about money every day, or *any* day for that matter. That didn't mean I was going to live like a crazy, wild person; it just meant it wasn't going to rule every decision in my life. Most people's financial plan is based on developing some type of security. Let's assume that's your dream. The next question you have to ask is, "What does financial security look like?" What monthly amount or level of assets is required for you to feel financially secure? Do you need to be making $60,000? Do you need to have $50,000 in savings? That's Step 1. If you have your dream and goal, what's the plan? What steps do you need to take to get there? Is it possible in your current situation? You have to be realistic or find a new path to get there. If you're flipping burgers at McDonald's, I don't care how many burgers you grill, it's going to be difficult to get to your goal, and therefore, you're not going to reach your dream. Maybe you have to start a small business on the side or get a second job. What daily, weekly, or monthly activity will it take to meet your plan to attain your goal?

When I put those six numbers on my screensaver, I had my dream. I wanted financial independence. I had a number in my mind that I needed to reach to step away from the business. I felt like I had the vehicle to accomplish that if I continued to stay down the same path I was on, calling on the next pilot and building the team around me to succeed. A few years earlier, Lisa and I had gotten into multilevel marketing at Amway, and while our purpose there was for personal development, we had achieved a decent level. By late 1998, we had reached Emerald status, meaning we were making somewhere between $75,000 and $100,000 a year. It was the final piece of the framework. When you set out to fulfill a dream, you have to monitor your effort. If you don't monitor your effort, you're not going to reach your plan, which means you're not going to meet your goal.

It's important to stop along the way as we pull our wagons down the path toward our dreams. Have you ever watched NASCAR and seen the lead driver pull off onto pit road? Those drivers use timely pit stops to review their strategy, make adjustments, and fuel up. You would think if they could, engineers would build a NASCAR vehicle that could just keep running forever. But that's not the way it works. The pit stops revitalize not only the car but the driver as well. Our lives call for similar pit stops. It's easy to get so caught up in the daily grind that we lose sight of our goals or the planned road to reach them. Sometimes you have to sit back and view yourself. Sometimes what you have to do is stop the wagon altogether and take an audit of where things are. Are you really going where you want to go? Maybe you're making progress, but have things changed? No matter where you are in the race to your goals, sometimes you have to pull over, take a break, and get a tune-up to avoid going off the track.

On December 31, 1998, I stepped away. I had called the owner-ship group and they agreed to buy out my 10 percent interest for $1 million and hire me at a six-figure consultant fee for one year. If anybody had told me that when I first started, I would have said that's a great deal. I just couldn't see that far out. When I left RAA, we had $500 million under management, and I'd probably brought in $350 million of it. A lot of people close to me said, "You're making a mistake. You can make a lot more money just staying at RAA." All of that was likely true. It was probably a terrible financial decision and likely cost me $10 million through the years. I could have stayed and accumulated more, but I had an idea of what was enough and had reached that goal. Also, I felt comfortable that Scott Frost and another partner, Jeff Prendergast, could work together and operate the company as well as I had done, if not better. They proved me right. I would never trade those eighteen months for any other time in my life. I spent the next year and a half, from the end of 1998 to May 2000, enjoying time with my family. Justin was a golfer on the high school golf team, so I spent as much time as I could going to his practices and traveling to his tournaments. As I look back on it, there's no amount of money I would take in exchange for that time with my family.

The thing about goals and dreams is that if you don't have another big thing before you reach the finish line, it's hard to go beyond it. Once I got to the point where I thought we were comfortable financially, I struggled with that myself for a while. *What's my next thing?* I was still too young for the answer to be "nothing." Is that all you got? I thought about my mom and dad. They were the first ones in their families to graduate from college. What happened? They got their big thing and then life took over. They never reset and aimed for the next dream.

Setting Out for the Next Opportunity

I didn't know what was next, but I knew $1 million wasn't going to be enough to last forever. It sure seemed like a lot of money, but I had just turned forty years old and had to push forward to find life's next blessing.

I never lacked for opportunity, but it wasn't my family name, my parents' fortune, or anything like that got me there. I certainly believe God was a participant in all of it, but I also believe that I took what God gave me and used it, not always perfectly, but certainly with righteous intent. I was continually trying to work on ways to get better at what I was doing, whether I was at Murphy Oil, RAA, or in my personal life. Sometimes in life, we have to create our opportunities. You can't expect them just to come. When we don't have a dream, we find ourselves moving in place in life. It's the people who have nowhere to be who get stuck. When you pull your wagon across one milestone, do you stop? We have to be open to opportunities because if you stop looking, they'll pass you by and you'll wake up one day in the same place wondering where the heck time went. Certainly, after eighteen months off, I needed to be open to whatever was next in my life.

God certainly had a plan for my next step, even though I didn't have it on my radar. A month or two after Justin went off to college, I received a call from a good friend named Bart Roberson at AMR Investments, the subsidiary of American Airlines that had been so impactful on my career. "Hey," he said. "Do you want to get back into business?" I had helped Bart land his job at AMR years earlier. Bart (who was referred to me by one of our friends from First Baptist Dallas) had come to me looking for a job at First Southern Trust, but we had just launched the venture and weren't hiring. I referred him to AMR Investments and he'd been there ever since. After I left RAA, while the company carried on successfully, management made some changes and began pulling money away from the AMR mutual funds and investing it elsewhere. I had stayed pretty loyal to AMR over the years. We didn't use their mutual funds exclusively, but we had invested 70 percent of our funds with them. They felt they had essentially put us in business, which they had, and with a diversified group of investment options and investment managers, RAA was certainly meeting its fiduciary duty to its clients when it utilized AMR. They had always stood by me and that was a big deal. They weren't happy that RAA investments was going away, and Bart asked if I'd help them start a new company. "I'm not starting another company," I told him. "If you want to buy a company that's already established, I'll help you do that." So in 2000, AMR hired me as a consultant, and we began searching.

The first company we tried to buy was RAA, but they didn't want to sell—or at least they didn't want to sell to us. We tried and tried, and I thought we were going to come to a deal, but we just couldn't make it happen. I'll never forget sitting at a meeting at the Riviera Country Club with AMR and Metropolitan West, our other partner, and the head of MetWest said something that helped me. "You can spend your entire career trying to buy somebody that doesn't want to be sold, and you can justify it all you want, but that's where we are with RAA." He was right; it was time to look elsewhere. They were probably using us as leverage. Not long after they sold to E*TRADE, which again will become ironic as you'll read later in this story.

I found out later that Bill, Jim, and Rick weren't happy that I had taken a consulting assignment with AMR. They wanted to sell—but not to me.

I wasn't sure if they were interested, but the number two company in the pilot investment business was Pritchard, Hubble & Herr (PH&H). You probably know what I'm going to say. What was their big mistake? They named the company after themselves. Now the Pritchard of the group was retiring, and Herr decided he'd get out too. We had been tough competitors, but we were friendly. When I left RAA, Herr sent me a handwritten letter that was really sweet. "Ron, if you're ever interested in being back in business again, please give me a call," he wrote. "You were always the consummate professional." I told Bart we could probably make a deal. I knew enough about PH&H to know they weren't structured like RAA had been and, if we bought the company, I could change the structure so that the synergies would make it more efficient and profitable. PH&H agreed and by the end of 2000, we had a deal.

It hadn't been a year since the close of the deal when I received a call from the people at AMR and MetWest. "Look," they said, "this thing is not being run right." When we made the deal, PH&H had a horizontal structure where everybody was reporting to everybody. It was chaos. Things hadn't improved since the sale, and the investors wondered if I'd go in and fix it. Herr and Pritchard were gone, leaving one of the founders, Bill Hubbell, and two pilots, Kevin Dolan and Tony Desantis. I stepped in as president and CEO and made Bill the chief operating officer. Kevin and Tony were important pieces because they brought their friends in as clients, but since they split their time between flying and working at PH&H, they couldn't be responsible for day-to-day operations. So we named them both senior vice presidents. The goal was to look a lot like RAA. I had good relationships with the other partners, so it wasn't as hard for me as it might have been for others. We shared a mutual respect for one another; they knew I had been a big part of building RAA, and I knew they were responsible for PH&H. As the old saying goes, "Be careful how you treat your people on the way up, because on the way down, they're going to be stepping on you." I learned another valuable lesson: "Be careful how you treat your competitors because they may become your partners." You just never, ever know what the future might hold.

Somewhere along the line, MetWest decided it didn't want to be in the retail investment business dealing with individuals. I hadn't put any money up in the deal, so I only owned options. AMR and MetWest had paid several million dollars to buy out Pritchard and Herr. After I stepped in, our team got PH&H back on track. I knew it was going to make money. So I went to MetWest with a proposition: "Why don't I buy this from you?" They agreed that if I could come up with the money, they'd sell their share. AMR, meanwhile, agreed to carry the money it had put up as a non-recourse loan that we'd pay back over time. They were making revenue from the money we were investing in their mutual funds, so it was a good deal.

The only problem with the plan? I didn't have financing and didn't have more than a million dollars to make the deal happen. Instead, I devised a plan. I would come up with several hundred thousand dollars if MetWest would finance the rest. I may have been able to do it myself, but it probably would have taken all the money we had. I went to Bill, Kevin, and Tony. "Here's what we need to do," I said. "We're gonna put up several hundred thousand dollars in a

CD, and we're going to borrow several hundred thousand dollars, and that's going to get the deal done."

I can't believe the deal worked. They each put up the money and I put up what, in retrospect, turned out to be a pretty small amount. My investment bought 28 percent of the company but 51 percent of the voting interest. For a relatively small investment, I obtained controlling interest. Because I controlled 51 percent of the general partnership, I essentially controlled 100 percent of PH&H. I didn't flaunt it, but I knew I could get done what we needed to get done.

We were off on our own. While we had hit a lull in retiring pilots in the early 2000s, we encountered fortunate timing around the time of the sale. Delta Airlines hit major financial trouble and offered their pilots an early-out program, leading to an abnormally high number of Delta pilots retiring. When we split off from AMR and MetWest, we had $500 million under management. Within a year and a half, we had reached $700 million due primarily to the efforts of our vp of sales, Ken Mills, and his team. Everybody was making more than they'd ever made. We paid off our notes with AMR and paid off MetWest early. We had accomplished what we had set out to do. In pilot terms, we were cruising at thirty thousand feet searching for our next destination.

~ *Chapter 7* ~
A.C.T. (Action, Consider, Takeaway)

Action

List any major decisions that you believe were forced on you and summarize how you responded. Then list the things that have occurred in your life that appear to have only been able to happen by intervention of a power greater than your own. For me, as a person of faith, I believe there is no way I could have purchased controlling interest in a multimillion-dollar company for a very small amount of money. God was in the middle of that, I assure you. What about you?

Consider

Are you aware of what could be going on around you, or are you just pulling your wagon as fast as you can? Maybe it's time to be the cargo in some areas of your life and learn from others or be led by others.

Takeaway

Some of the most important happenings in our life occur when there is no way we could have actually scripted them in that manner. Realize that and don't let an opportunity pass you by—seize it!

CHAPTER 8

"Yes" Isn't Always Easy

*M*ore than three decades later, I still can't erase the sentence or the pain that followed from my mind. "Ron and Lisa," the school administrator said from across the table, "you need to realize that Daniel just does not have the gray matter that it takes to stay at our school."

Gray matter?! I was stunned and angry. Daniel was six years old and was so excited to start kindergarten and join his older brother, Justin, at our church's private school. Lisa and I knew Daniel had his challenges, and he had fallen behind his classmates in the first five weeks of the school year, but the administration wasn't willing to do anything outside of the norm to help. I've never been so hurt in my life, and I still can't think about that moment without tearing up. Lisa knew better than me because of her teaching background, that Daniel wasn't developing 100 percent the way he should. Maybe

I was naive, but I had hoped it would all average out at some point, that Daniel would catch up to his peers. The meeting with the school was a definite point of demarcation. It made me sit up and pay attention. That day I went from being a *pusher* to a *puller* for Daniel.

Daniel was born January 24, 1985, eleven days before I started my new job at North Dallas Bank and Trust. I left El Dorado for Dallas on February 3, driving through a rare snowstorm (yes!) to arrive in time for my first day of work the next day. It was during my drive west that Lisa's grandmother died. I received the call with the devastating news when I reached Texas. Lisa and I went back and forth on the phone deciding whether I should get back in my car and drive back to Arkansas or stay to start my new job. We landed on me staying in Dallas. A few days later, after the funeral, Lisa called. "Come get me," she said. That weekend I drove back to El Dorado to pick up Lisa, Justin, and Daniel.

Lisa had a feeling right away that something was different about Daniel. He didn't smile very much, and he had an unusual fear response whenever we put him on his back. His body would stiffen, his arms would flail, and he'd let out an agonizing scream. From the time he was just a few months old, Daniel would tense up whenever we approached the car for a trip. Once in his car seat, he would kick and scream. When we moved to Houston in 1986, with Daniel approaching two years old, our trip back to see Lisa's family in Arkansas lengthened to seven hours. One weekend we hit the road to El Dorado to visit Lisa's father and sister. Daniel began kicking and screaming immediately. We had been on the road for maybe forty-five minutes when I pulled the car over, got out, and opened Daniel's door. "Stop screaming!" I yelled. I shut the door, got back in the driver's seat, and kept driving. Daniel never screamed in the car again. While I am embarrassed to have yelled at a toddler, Lisa likes to say that God's intervention and a few forceful words from Dad produced a little miracle. Lisa was always keener than I was to how Daniel was developing compared to Justin at the same age or to other children we knew. Daniel was well behind, often by many months. I didn't think much of it, and the doctor calmed any possible fears with reassuring assessments. Overall, Daniel was a quiet child. Outside of when he was placed on his back, he didn't have many tantrums. He was very orderly. While most kids enjoy finger painting and other messy activities, Daniel hated them. He couldn't stand the mess. He did enjoy lining up Lisa's shoes in the closet or playing with his Matchbox cars.

The two things Daniel struggled with most were his fine motor skills and speech. When he started preschool, Daniel was one of the oldest kids in his class, but he clearly lagged behind his peers. Daniel struggled with things that were simple for other kids his age, such as buttoning his shirt or tying his shoes. The tasks that took focus and attention and required fine motor skills challenged him. Lisa was determined to teach Daniel to tie his shoes. All of his classmates could, and Daniel was frustrated. To make things easier for him, we bought Daniel Velcro strap-on shoes. He hated them. Daniel was left-handed, which only made things such as cutting with scissors or learning to tie his shoes more difficult. Lisa tried for weeks to teach Daniel to tie his shoes, even teaching herself to tie backward so she could show Daniel how to do it left-handed. Nothing seemed to work. One day, my Aunt Patty came to visit and happened to arrive while Lisa was in the middle of a shoe-tying lesson. Patty is left-handed and offered to take a shot at teaching Daniel. Five minutes later, Daniel was tying his shoes. We found out that while Lisa is right-handed, she had always tied her shoes left-handed, so when she reversed it in an attempt to help Daniel, she had actually switched to tying her shoes right-handed. It's a moment we can still laugh about today. For Daniel, it was an exciting accomplishment.

With the moments of excitement came stark reminders of Daniel's challenges. By age two, Daniel could still only speak a few syllables. He could say "buh-buh" to get the attention of his brother, Justin, and "duh-duh" to call our dog, Dudley, but that was the extent of it. We tried everything we could, but we couldn't get Daniel to talk. We found a speech therapist named Mary Ellen in Dallas, and thank God we did. Mary Ellen started working with Daniel three days a week and gave us a picture book that contained three-word sentences on each page. Slowly but surely, the work was paying off. After one year, Daniel began speaking in full sentences. As he neared the start of kindergarten, Mary Ellen suggested to Lisa and me that we get Daniel's IQ tested so he could get the best help possible. We scheduled a test at Scottish Rite Hospital for Children. We had been on the waiting list for seven months when we finally got in, just before Daniel was set to begin school. He went in and took the test. When the results came back, it was what we feared. The woman tried to offer support, but the scores she gave us meant that Daniel was considered "educable mentally retarded." The "diagnosis" said that Daniel would reach only a fifth-grade education level, that he shouldn't be able to dress himself or communicate verbally. Sure, Daniel had his challenges, but these were things he could do!

Daniel's scores didn't represent the Daniel we knew. The worst part was the results were going to get sent to the school. By the time the school received the test results, Daniel was five weeks into class. That's when Lisa and I got "the call." After I contained myself from the insult, I calmly asked for suggestions. The administrator said we needed to put Daniel in special education and that Daniel couldn't stay at the school past his six-week report card, just one week away. Lisa and I were devastated. We scrambled to find a Christian special education school—but it turned out many of the other Christian schools also weren't accommodating of children with special needs. Eventually, Lisa came across Oak Hill Academy. The school's kindergarten classes were full, but they were willing to start Daniel in their preschool class and assured us they would help him advance.

After Daniel settled into his new school, we took him to a children's neurologist, who diagnosed him with Pervasive Development Disorder–Not Otherwise Specified, also known as PDD–NOS. Daniel's disability didn't really have a name. Even worse, there wasn't anything we could do about it. There was no playbook. Lisa and I never thought about autism, which was rarely talked about in the early 1990s. Today, PDD-NOS is part of the diagnosis of autism spectrum disorder (ASD). After the doctor delivered the news, he told us not to expect Daniel to do normal things such as bike or skateboard. Lisa was immediately determined to prove him wrong. Not long after the doctor's visit, we went out and bought Daniel a bike. Lisa devised a plan to teach Daniel the motor skills and worked on exercises with him. After about a week of training, they moved to the grass and then the driveway. Within a month, Daniel was riding a bike. Lisa summed it up best in her book about our journey with Daniel, *I Would Have Said Yes*: "When someone looks you in the eyes and tells you what not to expect, don't just accept it. See for yourself what your child can accomplish. You will occasionally be disappointed, but mostly, you will be amazed."

What I've learned from Daniel is that when we say yes to the challenges in our lives, it isn't always easy. But it's worth it. As we pull our wagons along, there are cracks that throw us off track and cause frustration, but when we push on, the obstacles only make crossing the finish line more rewarding. Lisa and I never could have expected the challenges we would face when Daniel was brought into this world. We had no experience in either of our families with diagnosed disabilities. It hit us out of left field. How you deal with something in your life that is totally unexpected is defining. When things aren't going as you want them to, there is sometimes a limited impact you can have. I learned that the hard way. With a personality like mine—I see a problem, I fix the problem—it was very frustrating that I couldn't fix Daniel's problems. Yet we still have plenty of choices.

Lisa and I could have listened to the doctors and other naysayers and settled for the fact that Daniel just couldn't do some things. We were determined to prove otherwise. As Daniel's life continued, he developed that same determination.

There is no question that Daniel softened my heart. I remember when Justin was born like it happened yesterday. I can close my eyes and still see it. I knew the second he was born that I would die for him. I thought there was no way I had any more love left in my heart for another child. That was stupid of me! When Daniel was born, I loved him just as much. I learned when Allie Beth was born that each child holds a special yet different place in your heart. You won't love one more than the other, but each of them will be different. Many times in life, we don't have a choice in the challenges we face. But sometimes when things are the darkest is when God is most at work.

Lessons from Daniel

I don't know exactly when, but somewhere along the way we understood that Daniel could very possibly need to live with us the rest of our lives. If nothing else, we knew he would always need us financially and would need help with overall life management. Usually, we plan for our children to become adults, get "out of our wagon as cargo," and become the pullers of their own red wagon. Sometimes that just isn't the case; sometimes we have a lifetime of cargo that we must protect, while at the same time allowing as much independence as possible. Many times we would push, or Daniel would jump out of our wagon and start pulling his own, and we would think *Great!* only to have him need to be reloaded into our wagon as cargo—precious cargo—and be protected or helped along for a while. These moments are hard on everyone and emotionally challenging, but we must be prepared at a moment's notice to change our position in the wagon for those we care about the most.

After Justin graduated from high school and moved to Birmingham, Alabama, to attend Samford University, I decided to take Daniel on a ten-hour road trip to visit his brother. We made pit stops along the way and stopped at Lisa's sister's house in El Dorado to spend the night before completing our trip to Birmingham the next day. We were sitting around when her little boy rushed into the room. "I think something is wrong with Daniel," he said worryingly. More than a year prior, Allie Beth had come across the same situation at our home. She had walked into Daniel's room and seen him on the ground shaking, having a grand mal seizure. She rushed to Lisa to tell her. Lisa and my mother called 911 and Daniel was taken to the hospital in an ambulance. They performed blood work and a CT scan and determined Daniel was fine, that the seizure had just been a rare one-time case. This seizure was different. Daniel's eyes glazed over and he fell to the floor. We rushed him to the hospital, and the doctors performed the same tests. Since we were on the road, the doctor increased the dosage of Daniel's medication. We proceeded to Birmingham to see Justin, and the seizures continued during the trip. Daniel just kept smiling the whole way through it. Maybe it was God's blessing that he didn't really understand everything that was going on. It was good for me to be around when it happened. I'm sure Daniel gets down, but no matter the situation, he was always in a pretty good, positive mood. Daniel always had a smile on his face. Everything with Daniel showed me what's really important. Thinking about Daniel made me question, when I would get stressed or hyperfocused about a business-related issue, how important it truly was. *How important is this when somebody like Daniel has all the stuff going on that he's dealing with?* I saw that whatever challenges we face in life, someone else has it more difficult.

There were more fond memories of that road trip. Daniel loved cars so before returning home we stopped at the Mercedes-Benz plant just outside of Birmingham, where they made the Mercedes SUVs. We toured the factory and then stopped at our favorite, famous barbecue place, Dreamland BBQ. The thing about Daniel, like a lot of kids with autism, is he'd learn all these facts and they'd never leave him. They just fascinated him. I was driving down I-20 through Mississippi from Vicksburg to Meridian, along the countryside filled with pine trees. All of a sudden Daniel spoke up. "Dad, they're never going to run out of oxygen here," he said. "Son," I said confused, "what do you mean?" "Well," he said, "trees make oxygen." Somehow he had learned about photosynthesis and it stuck with him. It was certainly something I would never think about! God taught me through Daniel to be calmer, more patient, and to realize the value in people no matter where they are in life.

It was an interesting time in Daniel's life when we returned home. We were struggling with his education and trying to figure out the best place for him. Meanwhile, Daniel's seizures only worsened. He started having seizures once or twice a day and went through a period where he had one every few hours as doctors tried to get him on the right medication. Near the end of fifth grade, Daniel's school requested a meeting with Lisa. The principal and Daniel's teacher sat down and told Lisa that Daniel had reached his learning capacity, that he wouldn't advance much past a fifth-grade level. Lisa wasn't happy, and Daniel was back to homeschooling for sixth grade. We went back and forth between sending Daniel to school and Lisa teaching him at home. After Daniel finished tenth grade at home, he approached Lisa that summer and told her he wanted to go back to school. During her search, Lisa came across Liberty Christian School, which was a college-preparatory school, but they had added classes for students with disabilities. The only problem was the school had two therapists who could take on six students each. They had already reached their capacity of twelve. They were looking for a third therapist to add more students. By the time we got home, Lisa seemed destined to do the job. It was an incredible sacrifice for Lisa, but Daniel had a school. At the end of the first week of school, I took Daniel to the first football game. There's nothing like Friday Night

Lights in Texas. As Daniel and I watched the game, I remember him looking up at the lights. "Finally, a team!" he exclaimed. All Daniel ever wanted was to be part of something bigger than himself. Now he was a Liberty Christian Warrior. Daniel graduated high school two years later in May 2004. It was incredible to watch him walk across the stage in his cap and gown. He had proven that anything is possible, that if you put your mind to something you can achieve it. Maybe the journey won't be as you anticipate or the outcome won't be what you first expected, but with enough willpower and determination, you can overcome life's challenges.

Changing the Definition of Victory

I've always been an independent person from the time I was a little guy growing up in Junction City. Maybe it's the middle child in me, but that's the way I'm made. For as long as I can remember, I've been goal-oriented. No matter what you do, if you work hard enough, you can accomplish it.

One of the things I learned with Daniel is, just because you want something and just because you're willing to do the work for it, it doesn't mean that's what's going to happen—especially in the timing you want it to happen. I grew up on the border of Arkansas and Louisiana, but we lived on the Louisiana side by the time I was a teenager, and in Louisiana, you could get your driver's license at age fifteen (instead of sixteen as in many states). I'm sure my mom and dad were scared to death, but it was the natural thing to do, and they let me do it. I've been driving ever since. Daniel is no different than you or me in a lot of ways. As a young man, he wanted to learn to drive. He saw his mother driving, his dad driving, and his brother driving, so it was a natural progression. In his mind, that's what he should do too. Daniel did a lot of things people had told us he couldn't. He learned to ride a bike, he started rollerblading, he graduated high school. Driving wasn't even an option when Daniel was sixteen because he was still having seizures and, even in his mind, he probably wasn't ready. But in his early twenties Daniel came to us and said he wanted to learn to drive. It scared Lisa and me to death in light of Daniel's autism and spatial-recognition issues, but we started looking at options. If we could figure it out, we weren't going to deny Daniel the opportunity. We helped Daniel with parent-taught driver's ed online, and he passed the written test. Lisa and I were too nervous to teach him on the road. We found a class at St. David's Hospitality in Austin. I still remember Daniel calling one day to tell us he had driven on the highway. It was an equally terrifying and proud moment to see how far Daniel had come since we were told he wouldn't even ride a bike. We hired a friend, Aaron, to give Daniel driving lessons. He'd take Daniel to a big church parking lot to practice. Finally, he thought Daniel was ready for the test. They went to the DMV, but Daniel took the test and failed. Daniel was still determined. About a month later, Lisa took Daniel to try again. As he pulled out of the parking lot, Daniel hit the curb. The car turned around instead of exiting the parking lot. Daniel failed a second time.

We had always instilled in our children to set goals. Daniel's goal from the beginning was to get his driver's license while he was still twenty-five. The second time Daniel failed the test was a Thursday. Daniel would turn twenty-six on Monday. Since the DMV wasn't open on weekends, Daniel had one last chance to reach his goal. Aaron said he'd take him early Friday morning. I still remember getting the text from Lisa, a photo of Daniel standing in front of the DMV holding his new Texas driver's license. He had accomplished his goal. I would always get frustrated when things didn't go my way quickly. In moments like these, Daniel has taught me perseverance and patience and that being accepting of things that don't always go in your favor is part of life.

"We must realize that we never know the future anyway," Lisa writes in her book. "It's easy to dream when we think of a perfect world, a world where all of our thoughts and abilities roll into one, and life is smooth and uncomplicated." Daniel could have been discouraged when week after unsuccessful week passed and he still couldn't tie his shoes. He could have been angry when he saw other sixteen-year-olds driving and he had to wait until he was twenty-five. It isn't easy when we hit challenges in our lives but see other people seemingly go forward with ease.

Sometimes in life, you have to change your definition of victory. I don't doubt God's ability to perform miracles, but I couldn't wait to be happy for Daniel to have a total healing miracle. It never would have happened. We would have lived his entire life just saying, "I'm really going to be happy when he quits having seizures" or "I'm really going to be happy when he makes a bunch of friends." If we define victory in certain situations as being just as we pictured, it can be very difficult to ever reach the victories we seek. There are many times when victory is black and white. But with a lot of things in life, if you have a predetermined view of exactly how victory is supposed to look, you might end up disappointed.

~ *Chapter 8* ~
A.C.T. (Action, Consider, Takeaway)

Action

Someone you know in your church, at work, or in other communities has a disabled child. Reach out to that family and ask how you can help. Maybe it's simply giving them a respite one night a month so the parents can have a night out; maybe it's becoming a friend to their child; or maybe it's just praying with them on a regular basis over the phone or in person.

Consider

Families with disabled children experience their own type of loneliness and isolation. Even if it isn't evident outwardly, it's there. For most people, the cargo in their wagon changes as they go through different stages of life. For families with disabled members, that one piece of cargo is always there requiring care—in addition to all the other cargo that might be in the wagon during that stage of life.

Takeaway

Life is not fair. This is nothing new but it is important. If we expect life to be fair, we will be regularly disappointed. Sometimes we need to change our definition of victory.

CHAPTER 9

Seek Out Mentors and Get Unstuck

I was getting exhausted as Lisa and I sat in the nosebleed section of the nearly twenty-thousand-seat Delta Center in Salt Lake City, Utah. I wanted to sit as far away as we could—like sitting in the back row of the church—so we could escape if we wanted to leave. We had made our way to the mountainous city for Amway's Free Enterprise Day after a friend talked us into signing up with the multilevel marketing company. I still wasn't sure about the whole thing. My eyes were growing heavy as the clock ticked toward 11 p.m. Coming from a traditional business background you'd work until five or six, and that was it. You were done for the day. These events didn't work like that. We had listened to speeches all day, and there was still an hour to go. *Goodness gracious*, I thought. I paid attention as much as I could.

Around 11:30 p.m., a guy named Randy Haugen took the stage with his wife, Valorie. I've never been the same since. Randy reminded me a little bit of Fonzie from the television series *Happy Days*. He had a different energy about him, like when a church preacher is talking straight to you. Randy Haugen was talking straight to me. He had probably given the same speech a hundred times, but something about it rang true with me. Randy was kind of a rough guy, a gearhead who had a high school degree and never went to college. He was a wild spirit who didn't grow up in church but was in the middle of Mormon Country as a non-Mormon. By chance, Randy had gotten involved in Amway through Don Wilson, who couldn't have been more of Randy's opposite. Don was as straitlaced as you get, a New Englander from Bangor, Maine, who had a Protestant background and was very mild-mannered. Don knew some businesspeople in Utah, and they had introduced him to Randy. Despite all their differences, they had synced up and Randy had grown his organization to more than one hundred thousand affiliated business owners. He was a plainspoken guy. You could look at him and say, "If he can do it, I can do it." You could really believe it. This was something I could relate to. It didn't have anything to do with Amway's products. It was all about the personal development system started by a beer salesman named Dexter Yager. I knew then that I wanted to meet this guy named Randy Haugen.

Our journey to Amway and personal development started in 1994, just as I had been named CEO of Retirement Advisors of America. Another pair of lifelong friends we met through First Baptist, Tex and Paula Grubbs, had joined Amway not long before and, in an effort to build their business, were going through a list of people they knew who might have a little bit of motivation and gumption about them. One day, Tex reached out. "Ron, do you want to have lunch?" he asked. "I've got a business idea I want to run by you." We met at a Chili's in Dallas, and he told me what he was doing. I had never been exposed to multilevel marketing before, and I wasn't sure I fully understood it. "I'm busy," I told him over the meal, "but if it will help you for me to sign up, then I'll sign up."

Tex gave me a First Night Kit containing two cassette tapes and a brochure, and we went our separate ways. I took the kit home, put it on the counter, and I'm not sure I ever listened to the tapes. A few days later, Lisa got ahold of them. She started listening to the tapes herself. All of a sudden, she came to me excited. I'd never seen her like that before. She had supported everything I did, but she had never been business-oriented in any way. It made me more interested in Amway. Lisa's excitement wasn't so much about the money. She saw it as something we could do together. In some ways, our lives were diverging. I was busy trying to build RAA while she was taking care of our three kids full time. We started down the Amway path and signed up for the Free Enterprise conference in Utah.

I not only heard Randy speak in Salt Lake City but, when we returned home to Dallas, I bought all of his cassette tapes (think old-school downloads on Spotify). We quickly were sold on the personal development philosophy. Before Amway, I don't know if I ever actively thought about mentors. Sure, Richard Lewis had been a mentor at Murphy Oil, and others had helped me along the way to become CEO of RAA. Some people would say to me, "Ron you've been so successful in the investment business, what are you doing chasing after these Amway guys that are successful? What can they teach you?" To me, it was clear: They were successful in something I wasn't successful in (yet). I wanted to learn. Just because I was successful in one area didn't mean I was great in other areas. Many people don't figure that out. One of the most important things I learned is that, as you go through life, you have to pursue mentors and people who can teach you a new skill. Sometimes that puts you in a place of being very uncomfortable, but it's well worth it.

Getting involved in personal growth programs through Amway was a life-changing factor in many ways. I learned more about fatherhood and grew in ways I had never even thought about. I let the books I read and the tapes I listened to become the guidance I had found lacking in parts of my youth. Most critically, I learned the importance of seeking out mentors. In the years after I met Randy, I sought out Dr. John C. Maxwell, Dr. O. S. Hawkins, and many others. I knew I could sit and be stagnant or I could go do something about it. And so that's what I did.

John has been an important mentor in my life and has taught me so much about myself and life's journey. Through his books, he's undoubtedly inspired millions of others too. Having mentors is a key part of John's teachings. He writes,

> *Mentors matter, and having the right mentor matters even more. You see, the right mentor expands your vision. They help you see farther and stretch your horizons. They help you see more by uncovering your blind spots. And they help you see clearly to discover your best path to success. That's why I've chosen mentors at every step along my journey. I can't see it all, I can't know it all—and neither can you. We all need someone to help us in our pursuit of intentional growth, and the right mentor helps you take massive leaps forward.*

People throw the word *mentor* around frequently, but what I learned from John is there are three things to look for in a mentor: They *know* the way, they *show* the way, and they *go* the way. Mentors are meant to walk alongside us, providing experience and wisdom to guide our life's journey. They've been through it and can help steer our wagon. But finding mentors requires intentionality. We can be guided in life only when we are willing to seek out that guidance.

Lisa and I would listen to cassette tapes with Justin, Daniel, and Allie Beth in the car, so they were learning too. It was helpful to better understand not only the people I worked with but even Lisa, our kids, and later people with other views. Although the extra income we made through Amway was nice, and later helped to allow me to step away from business to spend time with my family, what I really thrived on was its introduction to personal growth. I had big dreams, and I knew I needed to invest in myself if I ever hoped to make them come true.

Becoming a Mentor for Others

When Lisa and I first married, we lived on a small piece of land in El Dorado with two mobile homes. Lisa and I lived in one; fifty yards away, Lisa's cousin and wife lived in the other. El Dorado was a small city, and since Lisa's family was reasonably close, we'd see each other often.

Right around the time Lisa and I got married, her cousin, Mike, and his wife, Debra, had a son named Richard. Technically, Richard was Lisa's first cousin once removed. (Her mother and Richard's grandfather were brother and sister. When your mom had twelve brothers and sisters like mine did, you remember how that stuff works.) Although he's technically a cousin-in-law once removed, to me, he always seemed more like a nephew or eager student. Not long after Richard was born, our firstborn, Justin, came into the world. For the next couple of years before we moved to Dallas, as I worked my way up at Murphy Oil, we built our family and watched Richard grow too.

Richard's family consisted of solid, blue-collar folks. His dad worked at the chemical plant in El Dorado, and his grandfather worked at an oil refinery. Neither had any kind of college education, but they were the kind of good, solid people who do their jobs well and keep communities running. We didn't see Richard much after we moved to Dallas. As Lisa and I continued to grow our family,

Richard's family was growing apart. His mom and dad divorced when he was eleven or twelve. He still saw his mom after the divorce. But she was working through some issues, so he lived with his dad, who raised him well.

As we started to develop our Amway business and think about a list of people we might want to talk to, Lisa couldn't get Richard out of her mind. He was now about nineteen years old—the same age as I was when I got started at Murphy. He had gotten married to a young woman, Toni, and they had a beautiful new baby daughter, Taylor. They were living in a little duplex that his grandmother owned. His mom was still dealing with her issues, while his dad had remarried and gone on with his life. Richard's family loved him and supported him as best they could, but from personal experience, I knew there wasn't a lot of upward potential for him in El Dorado. Lisa and I still had a soft spot in our hearts for Richard, and I wanted to see him succeed. He had a beat-up old pickup truck and a worn-out push mower. He'd load it up in his truck and take off at daylight to start mowing lawns. Every night he'd come rattling up the driveway, tired from a hard day of physical labor. This was his primary source of income, but it barely paid the bills. Toni's parents helped out whenever they could, but I knew Richard wanted more for his life than relying on his in-laws. Richard came from a broken home and grew up into adulthood doing the best he could. But sometimes even that is not enough. When I'd hear about Richard after Lisa talked to someone from back home, I couldn't help but think, *He's about to be stuck.* I wasn't exactly thinking about red wagons at the time, but if I had been I would have described Richard's wagon as hanging halfway off the cracked sidewalk, buried axle-deep in mud, overloaded with the burdens of youth and inexperience, and with no strong hand to pull it forward to a smoother road.

Lisa and I saw a little bit of ourselves in Richard and Toni. We, too, were young when we got married. We had kids relatively early in life. We grew up in the same small town with limited opportunities. Like Richard, I understood what it felt like when your parents split up. We didn't have anybody pulling our wagon at the time. We were trying to pull and push at the same time. We had a wagonload of dreams, the naivete of youth, and just enough stubbornness to make them happen, but the road ahead is tough when you don't have a guide. One weekend as we were driving back to Arkansas for a family event, Lisa called Richard and Toni and told them we'd like to take them to dinner. When we pitched the idea of joining our Amway business that night, they were interested. They looked up to Lisa and me and could see that we had changed the trajectory of our lives. Many people approach multilevel businesses the wrong way. They try to gather as many people as possible in their organization in hopes of making more money. We did the opposite. We pitched people on the personal growth potential and let them make their own decisions. This is how we led the conversation with Richard and Toni that evening. The personal development side of the business was what we liked most. The access to books, workshops, speakers, and events had opened my eyes to a world of possibilities, and I wanted the same thing for Richard. Lisa and I were growing, and I knew that, in a sense, I had gotten out of my small-town mindset and started thinking bigger.

The first thing we asked them to do was come with us to a big weekend conference in Houston that was just a few weeks away. This wasn't a small ask. Houston was more than three hundred miles away by car. Bless their hearts; they decided they were going to do it. We left that night encouraged and excited about the road ahead. It felt good to put a guiding hand on Richard and Toni's wagon and help them steer it toward a better path. We kept in contact with Richard over the next few weeks and sent him some books to start reading. He was cautiously excited about what he'd learn in Houston. Then their wagon began to veer off course. Lisa got a call the day before they were supposed to leave. Toni and Richard had gotten into a big argument . . . and they weren't coming to Houston. Lisa went into action and listened while Toni laid it all out. Sometimes guiding someone's wagon means putting out a stabilizing hand when it seems about to tip over. This was Lisa that day. She pleaded, explained, and encouraged Toni and Richard to come anyway. She didn't want a fight they would soon forget to derail the potential this weekend would have. They finally agreed to come. They may not be speaking to each other when they got there, but they would keep the promise they'd made to us. True to their word, they made the seven-hour car ride in total silence and arrived in Houston that Friday night. That weekend, they heard things they'd never heard before. Richard leaned forward in his seat intensely jotting note after note from each speaker. He was soaking it in like a sponge. They heard stories of encouragement and community. They heard how people's lives were changed, how relationships were improved, and how a business could be built. I glanced at Lisa and gestured to Richard and Toni. It was powerful to see these two kids change before our eyes. The future suddenly had potential, and they were looking forward to embracing it.

Richard and Toni became absolute students of personal growth. They were willing to listen and learn. They never thought they knew it all. They did the work to grow themselves and their business. Whatever it took, they were all in. Most important, though, they were willing to accept that no matter what their background was, they could advance. The past would not define their future. They were young, and neither one of them had a great education, but they were smart. Toni's mom owned her own bakery, so Toni brought an entrepreneurial mindset since she had seen firsthand what it took to run a business. Richard was great with people. He was polished and could put whomever he was talking to at ease.

Probably the most important decision Richard and Toni made was to pick up their little family and move to Dallas. They found a small apartment about a mile from our house and settled in. Before leaving El Dorado, Richard leaned into his creative nature and got an associate's degree in CAD (Computer Aided Design). Not long after they moved to Dallas, with the contacts he made in his Amway business, he got a job at a local architectural firm. Within a year or so, Richard had gone from mowing lawns in south Arkansas to working at an architectural firm. He was attending Amway events and learning, growing, and making new connections. Step by step, his road ahead became clearer and smoother. His wagon rolled a little steadier. He had a path forward.

One of those connections was Tyson King. Tyson was a former all-conference linebacker who played for the University of Texas in the mid-'90s. Tyson and Richard met through mutual acquaintances, and Tyson took notice of how good Richard was with people. Tyson ran an investment company helping teachers invest their pensions, and he asked Richard to come to work for him. As flattered as he was, Richard wasn't an investment person and wasn't sure he had what it took to make it in that industry. Tyson looked him in the eye and said, "You don't have to be an investment expert. You have to know about people."

So Richard left his position at the architectural firm and went to work for Tyson. With the permission of the school, they'd go in and talk to the teachers. They'd show them how to invest their money in the retirement account that the school system offered.

It didn't take long for Richard to become one of their top salespeople. Because of his personality and his earnestness, he clicked with the teachers. He had enough of a good old boy personality that people got comfortable with him. But he didn't come across as pompous either. Once again, Richard had taken the next right step toward his goals. He did well, but he was still keeping an eye on the future and looking for the next open door to walk through. It turns out I was that next door.

We were in growth mode and expanding our team at RAA, so I approached Richard and asked if he'd be interested in coming on board with us. I was proud of what Richard had accomplished so far, and I thought there would be a natural bridge between helping teachers and helping pilots. I'd also encouraged Richard to finish his bachelor's degree so he enrolled at Liberty University and began taking classes online. It didn't matter too much to me if he had that degree, but I knew not having it might stop him from future possibilities. My idea was that Richard would become a financial advisor (selling the services of RAA). This position would mean that he would be representing a firm that offered investment advice to clients so he would have to pass his Series 66 exam. This exam was created by the North American Securities Administrators Association (NASAA) and administered by the Financial Industry Regulatory Authority (FINRA). The exam has one hundred multiple-choice questions and requires a pass rate of 73 percent. It's a closed-book exam, and most people study for months before taking it.

We put Richard through training, and he put the work in and studied hard. When he got his score back, the news wasn't good. He hadn't passed the exam. Richard was smart, but some people simply aren't good test-takers. For whatever reason, the test tripped him up. We still had plenty Richard could do just short of offering investment advice, so we kept him busy making calls and setting up appointments. Richard was disappointed, but he agreed to keep studying and working for the next window when he could take the test again in six months. But the test day came, and the results remained the same. Richard still hadn't passed. While it was a setback for Richard, it was somewhat of a setback for me as well. I had vouched for Richard to my partners. I was just as shocked as anybody when Richard didn't pass. But I believed in him. By this time, Richard had endeared himself to everyone in the office. Everyone loved him and liked the work he was doing for us. Even my business partners, who I worried might be wondering what I was thinking when I vouched for Richard, were solidly in his corner. We all wanted him to succeed. We knew he'd be a natural if he could get out there and sell, but he had to pass that test.

Everyone felt bad for Richard. We'd all seen the hard work he had put in studying for the test while doing everything he could to help the firm and our clients. He was an asset, so we were determined to find something he could do that would support his family, keep us in the good graces of the Securities and Exchange Commission (SEC), and help Richard use his natural gifts. We ended up moving him to our Client Services Support department. It was disappointing to Richard, but there wasn't much else we could do at that point. I could tell Richard was frustrated. After all, he had ideas in his head about moving beyond financial mediocrity and building a different kind of life. He had these ideas because we had put them there. We had painted a brighter future, and now he was bumping up against a present obstacle. He was up against this exam that he couldn't find a way to pass, and it seemed to be closing the door on his future. His wagon was getting onto some bumpy roads, and whoever had the handle wasn't going where Richard wanted to go. He was in danger of tipping over and falling apart far short of his goal. He hit the books again and kept studying. I probably let my emotions affect how I was mentoring Richard. Finally, it was time to take the exam a third time.

No road to success is ever straight, and when Richard got the news that he still hadn't passed, it seemed like his road was about to change. Honestly, I'm not sure what I would have done in his situation, but Richard grieved and then kept moving on. What choice did he have? The road to success doesn't stop just because you get stuck.

We expanded his job as much as we could. But in the end, Richard knew he was going to have to take control of the handle of his wagon if he hoped to take it where he knew he could go. If anything, these three failures only served to stoke the fire inside of Richard. I knew he was far from done. I wasn't sure how, but I believed his best days were still ahead. In some ways, I failed Richard as a mentor because I tried to put the proverbial square peg in a round hole. Richard was certainly made to deal with people, and I thought since our investment business dealt with people he should be in the investment business. How wrong I was. None of this was Richard's fault—he did all that he was asked to do and more. It was me, not realizing the uniqueness about Richard and his strengths.

After that third unsuccessful attempt at the Series 66 exam, Richard changed course. For Richard, that came in the form of his network of connections. He was introduced to a new multilevel marketing company, and he reached out to Tyson King to discuss. Tyson was intrigued. Richard had already proven his ability to connect with people through Amway and the financial services businesses. This could be just one more step on his journey. Richard continued to work in the Client Services division of our company, but he took the energy he'd been using to prepare for the exam and directed it into this new opportunity. For whatever reason, this time everything clicked into place. His side business absolutely took off. He'd been moderately successful before. But after a couple of years, he became one of the fastest-growing team members in his new business. He was making more on this business than he was from his salary with me. One day he knocked on the door to my office and asked if he might have a word with me. He walked over and sat down in the chair across from my desk. He looked completely at ease. "Ron, I think I can grow my business even faster if I don't have to be here eight hours a day. I think it's time for me to go." I was hesitant. I'd seen people leave their day jobs to build their side businesses before they were ready, and they lost their stability. I didn't want that to happen to Richard, but he'd thought it all through and presented a rock-solid case. After following mentors for more than a decade, Richard was ready to take the handle, start pulling, and lead his own charge. Thanks to his perseverance and willingness to learn, accept correction, and push forward, he'd changed the trajectory of his life.

Richard was good at knowing when it was time to take the handle. With his family, he put a firm grip on it from day one, even though he didn't know where in the heck he was going. He took the handle because he knew he had that responsibility. In his career, he didn't try to grab the handle too early, which is a mistake too many people make. When Richard grabbed the handle and went off on his own, he was ready. At his core, Richard is a guy who listened to the principles of the red wagon and put them to work. He knew when to focus on family and when to focus on career. He took responsibility for his life and actions, and then he stepped forward with confidence. Anytime he got stuck, he'd find another way forward. Sometimes that meant asking for help. Other times it meant figuring it out on his own.

Lessons Learned Through Amway

Lisa and I were in Amway from 1994 to 2007. It was a fortunate time in our lives. We had some success financially, but the real success was getting turned on to personal growth. I had never even thought about it before.

We fell in love with some of the people, with the stories that were told, and the mentorship we gained and, in turn, provided. Our business grew to a point where we were the ones going around speaking at conferences. To me, Amway was like a worldwide dream builder. It made you dream, both big and small. I remember listening to a speech from Bill Florence, who had grown up in Athens, Georgia, and attended Georgia Tech. He was a clean-cut, country club kid who flew in the Air Force and was a master at self-deprecating humor. At one of his speeches, he held up his keys and went through each one, relating it to something in life. It was such a unique way to communicate. Bill was a sports guy. Maybe it was silly, but I turned to Lisa and said, "One day, I'm gonna play golf with Billy Florence." She must have rolled her eyes. "Are you kidding me?" she said. "You don't even know him. We're not gonna get to know them. How would that ever happen?" Today, Billy and I have probably played golf together a hundred times. That was a lesson I learned: I pursued those people. I didn't just meet them by happenstance. I could have gone my entire Amway career and not ever met Randy or Billy. Billy wasn't a part of our organization, and Randy was so high up that our business didn't matter to him.

Everything you do in life requires intentionality. It's important to remember that you are the one who defines your finish line. For me, when I was at Murphy Oil, I knew I could build a decent career, but it would be far short of the goal I'd set for my life. That's when I knew I had to move. Richard's story was different. He had come a long way from a duplex rented from a family member, a run-down pickup truck, and a sputtering lawn mower, but he still was far from where he expected to be.

Perhaps you can relate. Maybe you started in a small town with big dreams but no idea how to make them a reality. You might have been fortunate enough to have a mentor or someone who saw something in you that you didn't notice yourself. Maybe that's where you find yourself right now—with a head full of dreams but no idea how to pursue them. You might feel stuck in a rut. It may be one of your own making, or it may be one that's based on where you were born, who your family was, your health, or a host of other reasons. It could be that, like Richard, you are doing a job that you enjoy, but at the end of the road it won't get you where you want to go. Changing tracks takes courage. It requires walking away from what you know into an uncertain future. It involves leaving the comfort of familiarity for the discomfort of the new. It may get better, but only after it stretches you and pushes you past your point of comfort.

Or maybe you're living someone else's dream. Maybe a well-meaning parent held you too close or pushed you too far, and now you find yourself doing something that doesn't light you up or excite you. It may pay the bills and keep you busy, but deep down you know that you aren't really controlling your destiny—you're simply along for the ride.

The truth is that many people reach a certain point in their lives and sort of set life on autopilot and hope to coast the rest of the way. Unfortunately, you can't do this for long, or you'll quickly find yourself moving backward. There are too many forces pushing against you to simply sit still. When you work to take charge of your life, you discover another way. Instead of feeling stuck, you feel liberated. Where you once felt directionless, you now clearly see the way forward. No matter what's happening in your life, there is always room to learn. If you're willing to pursue dreams and goals, you can find the guides that help you see what you can't see on your own and lead you to a better tomorrow.

~ Chapter 9 ~
A.C.T. (Action, Consider, Takeaway)

Action

Write down these words:

- Financial
- Career
- Relationships
- Spiritual

Who are your mentors and/or coaches in each area? You may have other categories as well that are important to you, such as health and wellness.

Consider

Have your mentors accomplished something you desire? If so, which of their accomplishments resonate most with you? If they haven't, then we need new mentors.

Do you spend time with your mentors efficiently, with a purpose?

Takeaway

Find mentors and coaches. Seek them out. Value their time. The type of mentor you need in the various areas of your life might change over time.

CHAPTER 10

Change Your Method,
Not Your Message

*A*s Pritchard, Hubble & Herr (later merged with RAA) soared, growing by as much as $200 million per year in the early 2000s, people started coming to me with new ideas. Why don't you take what you're doing with pilots and do it with everybody else? Every time I was asked, I resisted making the move—and it was the best decision I made. Pilots were what we knew. It was our lane. Until we talked to every pilot on this earth, why would we change that? I know people saw the opportunity to reach more clients and make more money, but it didn't get us to our bigger picture. Sometimes in life, we have to say no to a lot of good opportunities. Pastor O. S. Hawkins told me once, "Ron, here's the deal. You can change the method, but you don't ever change the message." That's the stance I took.

None of the other industries had the connectivity that pilots had, at least none that we found. We could have raised capital and tried both, but I didn't want to get off-kilter. We not only focused strictly on pilots but also had teams in our organization that focused only on American Airlines, Delta Airlines, and so on. I was always willing to listen to new methods to get things done and reach new heights, but if anybody wanted to change the message—if they wanted to make PH&H a leading investment firm, for example, and advertise that we were always going to have the best returns—that wasn't acceptable. That's not who we were. What we were was a company that knew the pilot retirement business better than anybody. If you were a pilot and wanted to be able to sleep at night, if you wanted to feel secure when the market went up and down, we offered that comfort. Through the years we had employees who would say, "I'm trying to sell new business based on our returns, and they're not as good as XYZ's happened to be this year." I always told them, "Well, you're going to fail because it's just not going to be that way." I would walk into hotel ballrooms where we hosted seminars for local pilots, and our salespeople would cringe when I took the microphone. "Look, not everybody in here qualifies to be a client of ours. Either we're gonna figure that out, or you're gonna figure that out, but the ones that do, here's what you're looking for." If someone was looking to double their money every couple of years, we weren't going to be the company for them. That would have been a message change. We were always trying to look at better methods without changing our message.

That same philosophy applies to our personal lives and our place in the little red wagon. The message might be the goals we set, and the methods are the ways we get there. As we go through our journey, our methods might change. We have to be willing to move to different parts of the wagon and push toward our goals in different ways. But we shouldn't abandon our goals or lower the barrier just because it's the easier thing to do.

There were reasons we didn't venture out of the pilot business. When you're looking at business opportunities, there are several essential questions to ask yourself. First, are you going to sell to the classes and live with the masses, or are you going to sell to the masses and live with the classes? In other words: Does your business have a niche attraction? Is it large enough that it creates business opportunity yet unique enough that it creates difficulty of entry? The answers for RAA and PH&H were *yes, yes,* and *yes.* It was extremely difficult for someone to walk off the street and enter the pilot business. Plus, there was the interconnectivity of pilots. During training at the start of their careers, American Airlines would hold classes of twenty or thirty new pilots at a time. American owned an apartment complex and housed all the pilots during their training. Even after they graduated from training, the airline held annual trainings based on your date of hire. So if you were in a class of twenty pilots hired at the same time, you were going to see one another again. The pilots bonded and formed lifelong connections. We just couldn't find those connections in any other business, even among doctors, dentists, or lawyers.

The trouble at Delta Airlines helped carry PH&H through the early 2000s after we broke away from MetWest and AMR. The airline's major cutbacks meant that instead of maybe sixty retiring pilots each year, there were several years where more than a thousand retired between 2003 and 2006. PH&H got more than our fair share of those. So instead of adding $80 to $100 million under management each year, we were growing at a pace of $200 million per year. My good friend and partner, Ken Mills, led this effort well as our head of sales. The timing was perfect. Our investment returns weren't any better or worse. Our system was a little more automated, and we probably got smarter, but who we were stayed the same.

Meanwhile, the future looked bright. That was the nice thing about the pilot business. We could always see into the future. After the dawn of the Jet Age carried the industry through a rampant 1960s, the oil embargo of the early 1970s slowed air travel and airlines hardly hired any new pilots. By the mid- to late 1970s, airline travel had returned. Going back three decades, we could see a surge in Air Transport Pilot (ATP) licenses in the late 1970s, meaning more pilots were about to reach retirement age—and our business opportunity was coming back around.

Trusting Your Partners

By 2005, as business boomed, I decided once again that I didn't want to handle the day-to-day operations of PH&H. Over the previous two and a half decades, I (with a lot of help from great colleagues) had built First Southern Trust, started Retirement Advisors of America, and revived PH&H. I had spent so much effort the previous five years getting PH&H to where it was. It was time to let someone else take the wagon handle.

For years I had worked with Bart Roberson at AMR Investments. Bart had been the one who asked me to come on as a consultant in what turned out to be the PH&H opportunity, but he wasn't one to take many risks. When we broke away from AMR and MetWest, Bart told me, "One day, I want to join you." I decided to go to Bart and see if he was ready. "Here's the deal," I said. "I need somebody to come in and run the day-to-day. I'll still be engaged with you, and I'll spend whatever time I need to make sure it's successful, but I just don't want the grind." Bart was ready to take the jump.

In 2005, we named Bart our chief operating officer and I transitioned to chairman of the company, acting as an advisor and guiding the operations. In many ways, Bart and I were the same. He was detailed and organized and good with numbers. I knew that even if I wasn't around, Bart was going to represent me well because his incentives aligned with mine. I still controlled the majority voting share, so at the end of the day I was able to say *yea* or *nay* on big issues, but of the 28 percent stake I owned, I sold 8 percent to Bart at a good rate. It was a good deal for me, too, since I had bought it for the right price. For Bart, he could see it as an opportunity to cash in big one day.

Not long after, in November 2007, an investment banker who knew Bart and me called. "Hey," she said, "are y'all interested in buying RAA?" After RAA had turned us down several years earlier and sold instead to E*TRADE, it faced the same questions I had fought against for twenty years. RAA didn't get nearly as much of the Delta Airline business as we did, and E*TRADE management was contemplating whether or not they wanted to remain totally committed to the pilot business or expand beyond it. E*TRADE had the business only for a few years, but it no longer fit what they were looking for. When people don't know your vision and your plan, everything starts being questioned and you end up having internal battles. You can show vulnerability by accepting and wanting more information to help you make the right decision, but once you make the decision, it has to be firm, and your top team has to go along with it. If not, they don't need to be on the team. A loss of focus or direction can be derailing. There was infighting between E*TRADE and management at RAA, and now they were looking to sell. "We're interested if we can figure it out," I told the investment banker. "How do we do it?" They wanted $20 million, all cash. With Bart still in the COO's chair, I jumped back into the day-to-day operations of the company, focusing primarily on the transaction opportunity.

The first thing we had to do was find the money. Luckily, through our own investment banker, Berkshire Capital, we found a group, Asset Management Finance, in New York. That group had come up with a model where investors would loan us the money at a low base interest rate, but one that guaranteed them a nice return if the company did well. They agreed to put up all $20 million. On December 26, 2007, we signed the letter of intent with E*TRADE to purchase RAA. By that time, both companies had around $900 million under management, doubling the company overnight and putting the newly combined total at nearly $2 billion.

We wanted to keep some of the management team from RAA, but most of them left. The CEO had already left. Upper management didn't like our deal, so they had gone to E*TRADE on their own to try to buy it themselves. E*TRADE turned them down. The way it works when you purchase another investment management company is each client of the company that's being sold must consent. If we wanted to keep that $900 million under management, it was going to take work. Luckily, the SEC allows something called negative consent. We could send a letter asking clients to either sign it and send it back telling us they were OK with the sale, send it back and tell us they were going with somebody else, or, if we didn't hear from them within sixty days, we could assume they had agreed to it. Of course, the contracts were at will, meaning they could leave at any time after that. In the end, most clients stayed. I think we had more than 96 percent of the clients agree to the merger. A lot of the people knew me already because they had been clients when I was there before.

Everything had come full circle. This was certainly another good reminder not to burn bridges when you leave one place of work for another or have a change in relationships.

Making Difficult Decisions

Bart eventually took over as CEO of the company, which assumed the name Retirement Advisors of America. Around 2010, I began having less and less of a day-to-day role. I was burned out.

We brought in a third partner, John Bentley, a friend and a college classmate of Bart's. I was available and paying attention, but I wasn't there much at all. They asked me to stay on as chairman of the board, which I was happy to do. I talked to the partners at least once each week and was involved in the board meetings and the company's big decisions. Otherwise, I was often on the road. Justin had graduated from college, was married, and was playing mini-tour professional golf in Florida; Daniel had joined a program in Austin, Texas, for young adults on the autism spectrum; and Allie Beth was off at college. So with our newfound independence, Lisa and I bought a forty-foot motorhome and hit the road. We visited the mountains and traveled to see our children. It was a grand time.

Back in Texas, the company was doing well. We were having nice distributions and adding more and more pilots to our portfolio. Seeing the success and enjoying my independence, I agreed to sell my control in the general partnership to Bart and John. There was risk involved because I was going from being a controlling member to noncontrolling, but, hopefully, they were calculated risks, as I was never afraid of taking a risk to get something done. That's why I had the majority control even though I purchased only 28 percent of the company—because I was willing to take the risk. I never focused on if it was going to fail. When I look at something, I try to evaluate the good and bad, but it's easier for me to visualize how things are going to be in victory than in defeat. Once I determined I knew how to make the pilot wealth management business work and could be a key part of building it from the ground, I knew if something happened, I could do it someplace else. I remember knocking on the door of a retiring pilot in Long Island, New York, as a twentysomething kid from Texas who grew up in Arkansas—younger than the pilot's own son—and yet gaining his trust to invest his entire life savings. That's where I got confidence. I knew people trusted me, and if I could do that here, I could do it somewhere else. It was a valuable lesson. At some point you have to have faith in your partners to take the handle. If you don't have faith in your partners, especially after you've been partners for a while, then you probably have the wrong partners.

At the same time, sometimes you have to follow your gut and take the steps you believe in your heart are the right ones to take, even when people close to you may not agree with you. That's tough because it's important to have your ears and heart and eyes open to people who are close to you, but sometimes you just have to decide. I knew I was done with the day-to-day management of the pilot business, but now I had to decide what was next. My mind wandered as Lisa and I traveled the roads across the country.

I remember hearing, "Some people die at forty and are buried at sixty-five." You can learn and grow at every stage of your journey, but you have to be willing. You have to constantly put yourself in uncomfortable positions to be able to receive those moments. If you stay comfortable all the time, then the teachable moments become fewer and fewer. But if you put yourself in positions and around people who create opportunities to make you uncomfortable, because maybe they know a little bit more than you do about something or they've had the experience you haven't had, you find yourself in new places. Hall of Fame football coach Lou Holtz said, "In this world, you're either growing or you're dying, so get in motion and grow." I could have easily remained there and run that investment company. I could still be running it today and still be clipping the coupons from it. When would I have quit learning? A long, long time ago.

It was time for something new. I just didn't know what.

~ Chapter 10 ~
A.C.T. (Action, Consider, Takeaway)

Action

If there were a sermon preached on your life or a TED Talk given, what would you want the title to be? Write it down, and then see if that title is consistent with where your life is now and where you are headed.

Consider

"You can change the method, but you don't ever change the message." Ask yourself if you've been consistent in your message about who you are and your goals to your loved ones, friends, and coworkers. Also consider whether you have been flexible in your methods or if you're more focused on doing something your way as opposed to your team (family, work, friends) accomplishing an important goal.

Takeaway

Be on the lookout for "shiny" objects that take us off message. Know the difference between a *message* and a *method*.

CHAPTER 11

Are You a Participant or a Crusader?

"Crusader or participant . . . which will you be?" I asked the crowd shortly after taking the stage in Phoenix with Lisa by my side. It was 2001, and as I settled into my business career, we occasionally traveled to different cities to speak. Through the first twenty years of my career, I had gone from the mailroom to CEO for a second time at a company with hundreds of millions of dollars under management. Even then I still had this question tugging at me: *How do I make an impact?* I wanted a message that would spark the crowd the same way.

There are a lot of people who just participate in life. They go along to get along. Maybe they stand on the side of the parade route instead of being in it. It's not that they're bad people or there's even anything wrong with it. The majority of people we come across in life are participants. But at some point, if you really want to move ahead, you have to decide whether you're going to be a participant or a crusader.

On the surface, participants and crusaders may appear very similar. A participant is a person who is a partaker, someone who takes part in an activity. A crusader is a person engaged in a crusade, a vigorous, concerted movement for a cause. The fact is, they're very different—just look at their synonyms:

Participant: assistant, aide, colleague

Crusader: nonconformist, revolutionary, reformer

The first way to know a participant is to look at the majority in anything in life—these are the participants. Participants are part of the team, but their goals are personal, and self-preservation is number one above all else. They see the challenges of the past as insurmountable obstacles of the future. They are afraid to commit. I remember listening to a TED Talk from Mel Robbins, author of the book *The 5 Second Rule*. The rule is simple: if you have the instinct to act on a goal, you must physically move within five seconds or your brain will kill it. Sometimes, getting what we want in life is as easy as deciding. The problem is, many people won't decide. "Your problem isn't ideas. Your problem is you don't act on them," Robbins says in her talk. "You've got stuff to do and it's not going to happen in your head." You have to decide to become a crusader.

You'll know a crusader in life when you see one. They are focused and battle ready. They are resilient and bounce back. When they fall, they are always looking up because if they can look up, they can get up. They understand the goal of the crusade and they have vision— they see the future. When I think of having vision in life, I think of Andy Stanley, the pastor of North Point Community Church in Atlanta, who said it best in his book *Visioneering*. "Everybody ends up somewhere in life," Andy writes. "A few people end up somewhere on purpose. Those are the ones with vision." But vision isn't enough! We can dream all day long, but can we follow through? As Andy writes, a vision gives our lives purpose:

> A clear vision, along with the courage to follow through, dramatically increases your chances of coming to the end of your life, looking back with deep abiding satisfaction, and thinking, *I did it. I succeeded. I finished well. My life counted.* Without a clear vision, odds are you will come to the end of your life and wonder. Wonder what you could have done—what you should have done. And like so many, you may wonder if your life really mattered at all. Vision gives significance to the otherwise meaningless details of our lives. And let's face it, much of what we do doesn't appear to matter much when evaluated apart from some larger context or purpose.

When we have a vision for our lives, it gives us a focus and a path forward. Every person on this planet wants to live a life that matters. They want their journey to be, if not epic, at least impactful. They want to do work that matters and make the world a better place. When their journey is complete, they want to know that they, and their lives, mattered. You may have the best of intentions, but without a vision and a plan they won't get you where you want to go. Are you leading or drifting? Are you taking the easy road or pulling into a more difficult path? Are you following the crowd or charting your own course? There is a difference between being a dreamer and a visionary. We can spend all the time in the world dreaming up ideas and things we want in life. It doesn't take anything special to dream. Vision takes courage and sacrifice. Visionaries can see into the future, plot their course, and remain focused on the goal. They have motivation and direction. Martin Luther King Jr. said, "The difference between a dreamer and a visionary is that a dreamer has his eyes closed and a visionary has his eyes open." You may start as a dreamer, but are you willing to become a visionary? You may be a participant, but are you willing to become a crusader?

The truth is you don't have to be special to build a life you're proud to live. My life has certainly proven that. Anyone can do it with the right motivation and enough commitment. When you know where you want to go, you can craft a plan to get there. You can anticipate the obstacles you may encounter along the way and ensure that you have a plan for when you reach them. No one wants to look back on life and have regrets. But that's what can happen when you don't have a plan in place or, to use my terminology, a guiding hand on the handle of your wagon. If you aren't careful, you can simply drift your way through life. That is no way to live! If you aren't intentional about where you want to go and how you're going to get there, you'll never experience the success and abiding joy of a life of purpose and value. Of course, there will be obstacles to overcome and difficult roads to navigate, but you get to choose your direction. Can you stay focused when you encounter rough patches? Will you get back up when you fall? Most important, when you reach a fork in the road and feel directionless, will you decide where to go next? Like anything in life, the results you get are determined by the effort you expend. Pulling your wagon is no different. When it comes to building a life of intention—one that is not prone to drifting—you set the course, but it's with the help of others that you reach the finish line. The most worthwhile things in life are rarely achieved alone.

Are you willing to take on the characteristics of the crusader in everything you do? We have enough participants in the world. We need armies of crusaders in all walks of life. More than anything else, crusaders attract more crusaders. In Mark 10:45 it says, "For even the Son of Man did not come to be served, but to serve, and to give his life as a ransom for many." There is no greater example of a crusader than Jesus Christ. He epitomized the characteristics of a crusader, proven by the fact that, more than two thousand years after he walked the earth, thousands of people each month join his crusade. Who are some historical examples of participants? There are none because history does not record participants. Who are some of the great crusaders in history? Thomas Edison, Henry Ford, Martin Luther King Jr., Abraham Lincoln, Booker T. Washington, Ronald Reagan, Winston Churchill, and the list goes on.

As I asked the crowd that day in Phoenix and have asked many others since—including at Liberty Christian School for Daniel's baccalaureate service in 2004—*are you a participant or a crusader*? I'll never forget walking off the stage in Phoenix with Lisa and meeting Daniel in the back room that day in 2001. He was sixteen and had listened to the speech. "Dad," he said, "I want to be a crusader." I did too.

The Call to Public Service

I sat in my home office on November 29, 2011, reading the *Dallas Morning News* when a headline struck me. "Solomons says he won't seek re-election to Texas House," it read. Burt Solomons had been the state representative of District 65 in Texas for nine terms, having won the seat for the first time in 1994, the same year George W. Bush was elected governor. After selling my controlling stake in the transformed Retirement Advisors of America, I was still searching for what my next move would be.

In my subconscious, I had always thought once I was comfortable with our financial security, I was going to do something with more significance. It wasn't that what I was doing with the investment businesses wasn't important—it actually created a lot of significance along the way for a lot of people—but whether it was public service, volunteering on the board of the Autism Society, or something else, I was looking for something new to make an impact in my life. When I reached that comfort level, something changed. I had accomplished the big hurdle that had always been in front of me from the time I left my parents' house at seventeen years old. *What are the things that are important?* I wondered. I had become engaged with John Maxwell's company as an assistant trainer and taken trips around the world to Brazil, Romania, South Africa, and more. I considered starting a new business. Then the headline in the *Dallas Morning News* hit me. I had always been interested in politics but had never been engaged with it outside of donating to causes and politicians I supported. I'd always wanted to be in the part of the organization that could make a difference and would have an exponential effect. Being one of 150 people sitting in the house of a state with twenty-seven million people certainly fit the bill. As I sat in my office it became clear to me that it was something I should pursue. I think God put that newspaper in front of me. I didn't know if I would win or lose, but I knew it was something in which I needed to be engaged. I went to Lisa, and she instantly agreed; it hit her the same way. When that happens, God is probably in the room. We decided to go for it.

I had been to the state capitol in Austin only one time, twenty years earlier to testify before a committee as part of a retirement investment association. I hadn't really spent any time in Austin. I didn't know any of the players there. None! There was a minister at our church who knew a few people in politics, and I thought he might know someone who could guide me. When I called him, he gave me the name of a guy in our Sunday School class, Pete Havel, who had experience in the lobbying world. Pete gave me the name of two conservative consultants. "Talk to both of them," he advised. So I did.

The first guy was exactly like who I thought a typical consultant would be. He told me about the political process and tried to sell me on using him. The second consultant wasn't anything like I expected. He told me to sell myself to *him*. I thought it was odd. Here I was, getting ready to pay him money, and he wanted to ask *me* questions. He wasn't just trying to get my business. He wasn't trying to sell me something. He was trying to make sure I was the right candidate. He knew this seat was open and he had his pulse on North Texas politics. When we finished talking, he was noncommittal. "Well, I'll tell you what, I don't know if I'm interested in taking you on or not," he said. "Give me a couple of days. Let me think about it." A few days later he called me back. "I'll do it," he said. "Let's have breakfast." And so Kevin Brannon became my political consultant.

When Kevin and I met for breakfast, I was clear. "I will do 100 percent of the things you ask me to do in this first campaign without question," I promised. "I will not question you. Whatever you say to do, whoever you say to meet, that's what I'm going to do." Sometimes when you feel like you don't know where you're headed, you have to ask someone else to take the handle of your wagon and lead. You have to go back to being a pusher for a while. When it's not your area of expertise, you need to find somebody that you're willing to take almost absolute guidance from. That's what I did.

When I decided to run for office that winter, I was fifty-one years old and had been CEO and Chairman of a company with billions under investment management. But even at that level, I knew I wasn't experienced in or knowledgeable of the political world. So I put my faith in Kevin and did everything he asked without question. The only reason I would question him was when I wanted to understand something. *You have to be willing to find your right place in the wagon, and it's not always holding on to the handle.* Most people think once they've held on to the handle of one thing in life, they should be holding on to the handle in everything they do. It just doesn't work that way. You have to be willing to be any part of the wagon at any particular time depending on where you are in life. You have to know when to let the handle go. That can be a powerful lesson, especially for people who are making a late-career move like I was. I had to change my position in the wagon. I had to just jump in and let others guide me. When I started the campaign, I had to be the pusher. All I was doing was going forward, following the leader.

It was a leap of faith, but I didn't have any other choice. If I had followed my business instincts in politics, I would have failed. While in business I could lay out the facts and make it happen; politics rarely works like that. It was maddening at first, but it's just the way it is. In the corporate world, I had to be willing to guide people through a plan, explain it to everybody, and find agreement from different angles. All I knew was that Kevin told me, "Look, you go out and you knock on enough doors of people that we know are going to vote, you tell your story, and if you do that then you're gonna have done everything you can do. Then, whatever happens, will happen." Kevin gave me a list of about fifty people in my county who he said were key influencers. He told me to call them and try to meet with every one of them. It felt a lot like my cold-calling days in the investment world. *Don't these people know who I am?* I thought. It was a stupid thought. It was just like I was a rookie. When Lisa and I went to meet with the Denton County chair of the Republican Party, I was met with blunt questions: "Who are you? And why are you running?"

While politics was an entirely new world to me, I found that campaigning was a lot like business. It was organized and we had a definite goal. It was either going to happen in my primary election in the spring and again in the general election on November 6, 2012, or it wasn't. If I knocked on enough doors and met with the influencers Kevin told me to, nothing was guaranteed, but I would have a good shot. First campaigns are unique. You don't know anything, you haven't been to the capitol, and you haven't said or done anything. It's a lot easier to make statements about what you plan to do and all the wrongs you plan to make right. I might not have known politics yet, but that was something I could do. District 65 in Texas is made up of middle class people. I knew it from my

because I didn't know the totals from Election Day. I called Kevin. "Hey, here are the numbers," I said. "What does it mean?" I'll never forget his answer. "It means you've won," he said. "They can't catch you, no matter what happens in the election today."

In business or almost anything else I've ever done in my life, other than the birth of our three children, I've never had the feeling that I had at that very moment. Kevin was right. I won with 59 percent of the vote. It was euphoric and satisfying. We had put the work in and done everything we were supposed to do, releasing the handle when necessary and taking my place as a pusher in the wagon, and the results had followed. I was headed to Austin determined to make an impact.

~ Chapter 11 ~
A.C.T. (Action, Consider, Takeaway)

Action

Make a list of people you consider crusaders, either throughout history or people you have known personally.

Consider

Look at the list above and think about what these people had in common. You have some of the same characteristics, I am sure of it. Which of those are your strengths?

Takeaway

Participant or Crusader . . . we can't be both in every situation. Decide where you fit. Look for a place to serve your community in an area that will require more of you than it will return to you. *This* is service.

CHAPTER 12

Get Out of Your Comfort Zone

I was in awe when I arrived for freshman orientation at the Texas state capitol in the final week of November 2012. I wouldn't become an official member of the Texas legislature until January, but I already sensed the gravity of the duty bestowed on me. I met forty fellow freshman representatives, the largest freshman class in thirty years, and found my desk on the House floor. I sat at my desk inside the state capitol that had stood since 1888. Inside the desk drawer was a Bible with the signature of every person who had ever sat at that desk. It wouldn't be long before my name joined them.

Before that happened, I set up a meeting with Joe Straus, the Speaker of the House I had been asked about frequently during my campaign. I didn't know yet what I would do when it came to voting for Speaker in January, but I knew I needed to meet him. The Republican establishment had gotten together before the election and, without any political background, I wasn't the traditional choice. But it was important for him to know my intentions.

"Look, everybody comes into this the first time as freshmen, but not all freshmen are equal," I told Joe when we met. "I come into this with fifty-one years of life experience. I want to bring my experiences in here. I don't know you; you don't know me. I'm not going to judge you right off the bat and I hope you wouldn't judge me. I'm coming down here to work. I'm not coming down here for anything else. I don't need the lobbyist money; I don't need any of that." Joe was a nice guy, but he was quiet, so I couldn't read him. I just felt like my approach was the right thing to do.

The night before we were set to get sworn in and vote for Speaker of the House, a representative, David Simpson from District 7, told a group of incoming conservatives that he was going to stand for Speaker the next day against Straus. David was a nice guy, and he was my deskmate during the first session, but there was no way he was going to get elected Speaker. He was too far right and wasn't going to have the votes. We stayed up late into the night on January 7, trying to convince him not to stand. We knew if he stood, he was going to lose, and we wanted to avoid having to take an unnecessary vote on Day One. I faced my first decision that night. If David stood and I voted for him, it would probably make my people on the far right happy. But I knew it was going to be the death of my legislative session if I voted against the Speaker on the very first day. Before balloting began, David withdrew and Joe was reelected. *That was a relief.*

At noon on January 8, 2013, I sat at my desk on the House floor, looking ahead at the 176-year-old flag from the 1836 Battle of San Jacinto hanging on the wall. It represented the 930 brave Texans who together went on a crusade for Texas's independence. Two days before that battle, General Sam Houston wrote in a letter, "It is the only chance of saving Texas . . . . We go to conquer. It is wisdom growing out of necessity to meet and fight the enemy now. Every consideration enforces it. No previous occasion would justify it. The troops are in fine spirits, and now is the time for action." In closing, he added, "My country will do justice to those who serve her. The rights for which we fight will be secured, and Texas Free." With a common goal in mind, Houston and his men rushed the Mexican army and, in an eighteen-minute battle, claimed victory in the Texas Revolution.

As the roll call began, I could feel the weight of the position I was about to accept. Secretary of State John Steen began calling off the 150 districts. Finally, he reached mine. "District 65, Ron Simmons." I raised my hand. "I, Ron Simmons, do solemnly swear, that I will faithfully execute the duties of the office of a member of the House of Representatives of the Eighty-Third Legislature of the State of Texas, and will to the best of my ability preserve, protect, and defend the Constitution and laws of the United States and of this state. So help me God." I was officially a member of the Texas legislature.

The interesting thing about arriving at the state capitol was I didn't know how everything worked. Kevin was my campaign consultant and, it turned out, he was just that. And although he tried to help me pull staff and other office details together, once I was elected this was a whole new part of the process. I realized I should have asked what happened next! I was scrambling. But I knew most of the people on the House floor, when they got started, didn't know how it worked either.

As I began pulling the curtain back on public service, I quickly learned valuable lessons. While there has long been a perception of polarization and a feeling that politicians don't care about you because you don't share the same beliefs, I saw the opposite almost immediately. What I found was most people involved in public service truly are in it for the right reasons. One of the most comforting aspects I saw about Texas, which extended across the entire country, is we really do have people who are willing to sacrifice to serve their fellow man and woman in a form of government. Even in the people whom I may have disagreed with on many policy issues, I saw their sincerity about the issues was just as great as mine. That was in contrast to what I saw in the media or on the campaign trail, which often lays out the idea, "If you believe this, you're right, and the other side's crazy."

Another thing I learned during my first 140 days was that accomplishing good public policy is hard. From the outside, it seems so simple. We often hear, "Hey, we ought to have a law that prohibits this" or "We ought to have a law that changes that." I definitely had many thoughts just like that before I stepped inside the House chamber at the capitol. I quickly learned there are at least two sides to every issue and, more often than not, there are three or four sides. That makes getting something done harder than people think. When you're involved in something that has such an impact—in Texas that means 27 *million* people—the system is designed to filter out the vast majority of those ideas so that only the really, really good ones, and the ones that have the persistence and staying power, come through. While that makes for better legislation, it can make getting things done a long, drawn-out process. I would have thought, *This makes sense. Let's just ram it through. We're Republican, we have the majority, force it through.* It doesn't work like that. That was a good lesson. It's pretty easy to stop something that's bad. It's the same way in public policy. There are a lot of stopping points where you can kill a bill. We live in a society where it's much easier to say no than it is to get to a yes and create positive change.

During my first session, there was a representative in my freshman class who earned the nickname Mr. No. The guy was against everything. He would literally vote *nay* and try to kill everything that came across the table. It was easy to do, and he could get reelected because there was no legislative history behind him. But he never got one thing done. When the time came and he wanted to pass a bill of his own, nobody would support it. "Why don't you support this?" he asked me. "You tried to kill six bills I had," I told him. It's easy in life to take the way out of saying no. It's much more difficult to do anything in life to get to a yes.

Finding Your Place

After I was elected as one of 150 representatives to serve the people of the second-largest state in America, I might have thought it was time to take the handle of the wagon. But it really wasn't. For different situations in life, we're called on to play different roles. During my early days in the political process, after receiving my instructions from Kevin Brannon I was often the front wheels of the action wagon, making decisions on when to change direction and where to go. Speaker Straus might be pulling the wagon, and I had to decide if I was going to be in his wagon or not. In business, once I had reached the top, if I wanted something to happen, it was going to happen. It didn't work like that in public service.

I've read John C. Maxwell's *The 5 Levels of Leadership* multiple times, I've heard him give talks on it, and I spent time as one of his assistant trainers teaching it and other valuable leadership lessons. And still, it wasn't until years later during one of his talks that it truly hit me: even when you reach one level, you're not at that same level in all aspects of life. That was true of my time in Austin. John would often say, "Leadership is influence." Maybe it wasn't exactly like business, but to be successful at the capitol, I needed influence. "If people can increase their influence with others," John writes in his book, "they can lead more effectively."

The 5 Levels of Leadership aren't so different from the wagon.

Level 1: Position—*People follow you because they have to.* Whether I was CEO of Retirement Advisors of America or state representative of District 65, my titles alone didn't necessarily make me a leader. My hard work in business and my campaigning in public service had earned me those titles, but it was up to me to get people to follow. As John said, "Nothing is wrong with having a leadership position. Everything is wrong with using position to get people to follow. Position is a poor substitute for influence." I may have had the title of state representative for the people of Denton County because of the 31,386 people who voted for me, but that didn't grant me influence. Whether I was representing my constituents or working with my colleagues, I couldn't rely on my title to get things done.

Level 2: Permission—*People follow you because they want to.* It's one thing to follow somebody because they're your boss and another to follow them because you choose to. John said, "Relationships with people are the foundation of leadership. If you're going to grow as a leader you have to grow beyond your title." If I wanted to get things done at the capitol, I couldn't rely on being a state representative or Republican. I needed to build relationships with people. I needed to get to know the other 149 representatives and, whether we were on the same side of the aisle or not, find out how we could get along and work together. I needed to listen, observe, and learn. I couldn't develop trust and influence without relationships.

Level 3: Production—*People follow because of what you have done for the organization.* I didn't run for public office for the title or the glory. I ran for state representative because I wanted to make an impact. I wanted to get things done. I had no intention of becoming Mr.

No. To become an effective leader, you have to be able to get things done and do things others might not. I like the analogy from John: "Too many leaders are like travel agents. They send people where they've never been themselves." I couldn't expect others to take a leap of faith, stand up for what they believed in, or join my cause if I didn't do the same. Could I face tough problems head-on? Could I make the difficult decisions that would make a difference?

Level 4: People Development—*People follow because of what you have done for them*. Not unlike a crusader, good leaders are able to bring people along with them. A crusade with nobody following is just a walk! In business, building an investment company into a multibillion-dollar business is about developing people and empowering them. It is about showing people the way, doing it with them, and then letting them do it for themselves. Public service wasn't so different—it was all about *teamwork*. Getting a bill across the finish line takes the ability to work together, show others the way, and compromise. It takes bringing people along. John said, "Successful people have discovered what they're good at. Successful leaders discover what other people are good at." Whether in business, public service, or life, getting things done is about empowering others.

Level 5: Pinnacle—*People follow because of who you are and what you represent*. Reaching the top of the 5 Levels of Leadership is something that takes persistence, intentionality, and longevity. Many people work to reach this level, but it isn't something that comes easily. Reaching the pinnacle in anything we do is about building a reputation based on what we get done. It's a level we strive for because it means that people will follow us not because of our title but because we do what we say and stand up for what we believe in.

You might be wondering what level you've reached. I've wondered the same thing at different seasons of my life. It wasn't until I arrived in Austin that I truly realized that I wasn't on the same level with every person I came across. Just because I might have been Level 4 at RAA didn't mean it transferred over or that I was at Level 4 in every area of life. That was an instructive lesson. I've had so many situations in my life where I was not the top leader but was a key backup to the top leader. Once I reached the pinnacle in one big area of my life, which was business, I was comfortable not being the top person. I had enough confidence to know I didn't have to be the number one person in everything. I could play a key support role and maybe even be more effective at building something great. It was like Ronald Reagan said, "There is no limit to the amount of good you can do if you don't care who gets the credit." Some people think you've made it only if you're at the top of an organization when, in some cases, it's actually much more comfortable and you're much more effective just one rung below.

Like me, you have to realize that you can't be the puller in every situation in life. If you're going to get somewhere, you have to decide you're going to get behind the wagon and push. It's about everybody realizing their different spots and knowing where they need to be at any particular time. If I had tried to pull the wagon when I really needed to sit back and be the cargo, I would have screwed it up. No matter how good a leader I was, I would have messed it up—I've done that and learned my lesson. At different times in your life, you may be called on to be any of these things: you may be the puller, you may be the pusher, you may be the cargo.

You don't always have to be the puller. If you try to be the puller all the time, you're going to fail. As John said, you have to realize you're at different levels of the 5 Levels of Leadership. Maybe you've been around for a long time and you're a Level 5 leader. If you try to be a Level 5 leader with every single person in your life, it's not going to work. We don't have the credibility to be a Level 5 leader with every person we meet. It didn't matter how successful I was in the thirty years before I was elected; when I got into politics I had to be the cargo for a while and learn. I had to go back to Level 1. Then I got out and pushed. Our natural instinct is to always want to be at the front of the line. The truth is, you can't always learn the best at the front. Sometimes you need to be in the middle. Sometimes you have to be in the back. And sometimes, people will ask you to be in the front of the line and you have to say, "I don't think that's right for me or the organization."

As I left the state capitol on my first day as state representative of District 65, I knew my place. I had my title, but my process was just beginning. I was firmly inside the wagon ready to learn, eager to begin the process. If you want to have a piece of coal sitting on your desk, you can go get it easily. But if you want it to be a diamond, it's going to take a lot of time and a lot of work to make it happen.

Meeting with the Members

When my staff arrived at the capitol for our first meeting after I was sworn in, I assigned them an unusual task. "I want to meet with every single member," I told them, "and I don't have an agenda." I'm sure they looked at me like I was crazy. I don't know why it came to me, but something told me, *Ron, you're going to work with these people down here.* I had met some of the House members during the election process, but I didn't really know any of them. I knew it was a relationship business and I needed to know the people. Even the people I may vote opposite of every single time, I needed to know who they were, where they came from, and what they were interested in.

Many of the aides would ask, "What does he want to meet about?" My staff told them there wasn't any agenda. They scheduled fifteen- to twenty-minute meetings with 149 House members and thirty-one senators during my first seventy days. I met with all of them in their offices at the capitol. *Every* one of them. Some were a little suspicious. I don't think anybody had ever done that before or has since. The meetings weren't long, but it was just enough time to let them know who I was and for me to get to know who they were. We never talked about policy unless they brought it up. I certainly didn't try to tell them anything about policy I was interested in, because that wasn't the reason I was there. In any situation, whether you're going to be a pastor of a church, running an organization, or part of an organization, you have to know what the heartbeat is. You won't ever know that without getting to know the people. What I realized through my campaign was that politics is a very personal business. If you were going to get engaged in politics, it was something that ended up being in your heart, not just in your head. I knew there was an emotional component to how we did our jobs, and being able to understand someone's emotional personality was just as important as understanding their policy personality. In some ways, it took me back to my sales days when I'd sit at the kitchen table or on the living room couch with retiring airline pilots. There were four keys: First, you have to be a keen observer of their surroundings. Second, do your research. Third, look for some kind of commonality. Fourth, don't do all the talking. Ask questions and then listen.

When I went into a representative's office, I'd look around. The decorations around the office and on the desk would tell me something about them. It was just like when I sat in the living room with retiring pilots. The pictures and items they had surrounding them told me a lot about their story. I also read up on them before I went into the meeting. What was their background? Was their district rural or urban? I wanted to be prepared and learn about them. After the first couple of minutes, usually spent talking about our families, I would pick up on something I had read about them or I saw in their office, because people generally display stuff that's important to them. It would tell me a little bit about who they were. Some of that came through understanding their family and what they did for a living or what their impetus to run was. That allowed me to connect with them. I tried not to talk very much. Meeting after meeting, no matter if it was with a far-left Democrat, a far-right Republican, or a moderate, I learned something new. I learned that they were people just like me. Their wife didn't like the fact that they were gone so much or their kids were crying at night because Daddy or Mommy was gone. I saw past their politics and realized I needed to treat them like human beings. I had to persuade people; I had to make sure that even when I disagreed with them, I wasn't disagreeable, because I might need them to help me on something down the road. Boy, was that a lesson I wish I could have learned in my real life before then.

So many of the meetings stuck in my mind, but I still remember sitting in Terry Canales's office. Terry was a fellow freshman from the Rio Grande Valley in South Texas along the Mexico border. Terry is Hispanic from a family of lifelong Democrats. I'll admit that I was naive. In North Texas, most of the Hispanic population was blue-collar workers who worked long hours at laborious jobs. I'd never spent any time around the Rio Grande Valley. As I sat and talked with Terry, it didn't take long to realize that the constituents in his district were just like me. They were doctors, lawyers, and business-people. It was a wake-up call. I wanted to slap myself in the head and say, "Gosh, Ron, you had a narrow view." Unintentionally, but I had a narrow view. Terry's family had come to Texas when the Spanish settled the land in the 1700s. They were called Hidalgos, and they were given these big land grants. Hidalgos were the people who built South Texas, and Terry was a fifth-generation cattle rancher. He lived on a ranch, grew up, and became a lawyer. I remember sitting down, and one of the debates coming up was gun related. Terry looked at me and said, "Ron, I'm a Democrat, but I want you to know, I've got lots of guns at my ranch. I'm a gun guy." That was another wake-up call. *Ron*, I thought, *don't prejudge people*. But in order not to prejudge people, you have to be willing to go out of your comfort zone and give them the opportunity to teach you something you don't know about them. Most people don't want to do that. In all my life, I'll never forget that moment. It was like, "Wow, Ron, that guy's more Texan than you will ever be. So don't ever disrespect that. Don't ever think that he doesn't know and doesn't care about Texas." Terry Canales was more Texan than anybody in the room. Maybe we wouldn't always agree on every issue, but there was no questioning that.

The benefits of my 180 meetings became apparent. If I had a bill up for discussion, or if there was something I was interested in, when I went to talk to a representative about a policy issue, it wasn't the first time I'd ever talked to them. I knew who they were, and they knew who I was. We treated people with a lot more civility. Even to this day, I have relationships with people I probably wouldn't have had if I hadn't gone and met with them.

Unless you reset your expectations and realize you're not always going to be the puller, you're not always going to be cargo, and you're not always going to be the pusher—you're going to get stuck. At any time, you have to be willing to take on each of those roles to get where you want to go. We go through life as a team. When we're willing to meet people at different levels and move around in the wagon, it allows us to get things done and reach the finish line. No matter where we come from, what we've done, or what we believe, we're always part of a team working together toward similar goals. It doesn't matter where you're headed; if you're willing to get out of your comfort zone, build relationships, and do the work, you can have influence. Even as one guy in a state as large as Texas, you can have influence on decisions that affect millions of people.

~ *Chapter 12* ~
A.C.T. (Action, Consider, Takeaway)

Action

Get involved in the political process of your community this year. Run for office, volunteer to help with a campaign, volunteer to serve on a municipal board or committee, attend at least two city council meetings or school board meetings in your community. Quit complaining and take action!

Consider

What have your life experiences up until now possibly prepared you for that you might not have yet explored (or pursued)?

Takeaway

Growth never happens in comfort.

CHAPTER 13

You're Either a Show Pony,
Plow Horse, or Workhorse

I hadn't really thought about it until I sat across from Joe Straus before I took office. "Ron, under the Texas Constitution, there's only one bill that we have to pass every session," he told me. "Only one. And that's the budget." If I thought I was going to come in and make things happen, that was my stark reminder of how hard it was going to be to pass legislation.

It didn't take long to learn that there were 149 other people who had ideas of their own and everybody wanted to get legislation passed too. Each session roughly four thousand bills are filed. Maybe fifteen hundred of those actually get considered. If you wanted to get things done at the capitol, you had to quickly decide if you were going to be a workhorse, plow horse, or show pony. In other words, are you trying to be somebody who tries to get attention all the time, or are you going to put your nose to the grindstone and work? Are you trying to be somebody, or are you trying to do something?

The Texas House floor is configured with a dais at the front center of the room where the Speaker sits. Below the dais is a podium with a microphone where a representative who may be laying out or presenting their legislation to the body stands to explain it and try to persuade the House to vote on it. Directly in front of them, about sixty feet down the aisle, is another podium facing the front. It's called the back mic, where anybody can get up and ask questions about a bill. I tried to have most of my conversations in private, but occasionally I would make my way to the back mic to ask a question. There were a few representatives who were on the back mic *all* the time. The podium had its own camera, and people could watch on the Internet. Mr. No was always on the back mic. There were ten to fifteen people each session who spent their time at the back mic. They were the show ponies. Pretty quickly, I could see that 10 percent of the legislature was show ponies. Another 65 percent were what I would call plow horses. They were good people, and they might pass some bills for their district, but they weren't often interested in tackling the big issues of the state. They needed to be led and directed and went only where somebody pushed or pulled them. They were valuable, but you couldn't lean on them for major issues and say, "I need you to go out and make this happen. I need you to carry this major piece of legislation." Then there was the remaining 25 percent who were really going to be the workhorses. They were there to work. I decided pretty early on that I wanted to be a workhorse. When I met with Speaker Straus, I told him, "I'm a workhorse. I'm gonna do the work."

When you went into a legislative session, the leadership—generally made up of the Speaker, Lieutenant Governor, and Governor—typically had a good idea of the major legislative agendas they wanted to happen. They'd look for legislators to carry certain pieces of legislation that were important, and they'd always be big, statewide-affecting pieces of legislation. The leaders wanted a member who was willing to take it on and help carry it across the finish line. They wanted workhorses. As one of 150 members representing 27 million people, I knew I had an outsize influence as a state representative. What I realized was that if you were willing to be one of the 25 percent who does most of the work, you had an even larger influence. The people who were willing to be serious policy workhorses could really move the dial on issues. I think that's true in any organization. If you're willing to roll up your sleeves and do the work and respect other people, there is a very small number of people like you who are willing to do the same. Therefore, you can have a great influence on what's done and what's not done.

Something I learned in politics is that when you lay yourself out there for others, it's never a part-time job. You may not be in your office full time, but public service is a full-time job if you're going to do it right. It makes you much more patient, and you become much more appreciative that it takes a while to get things done. The end result is prettier than the process. It's the same way with our lives, isn't it? What we may see at the peak of our careers or at the peak of our family doesn't encapsulate the journey it took to get there. It doesn't show the decisions we had to make or the challenges we had to overcome along the way. That's why there are really no "overnight successes" in life. When our daughters walk down the aisle and we've given them away and they're beautiful, that picture represents where things are at that point in time. But the process of getting there doesn't look like that picture. You have to realize that in order to get to that picture, the process can be challenging, it can be disappointing, there can be a lot of setbacks, but you'll never arrive at that picture without the process or without the journey. Life doesn't work like that. That's also why social media is so risky, because people think other people's lives are like they are on Instagram. We see the perfect photo—the highlight reel—but not the long, often grueling challenges of everyday life.

In 2015, Speaker Straus asked me to author and help carry a major transportation reform bill. House Bill 20 would completely transform how the Texas Department of Transportation operated in a key area: project selection. The legislation set requirements to more efficiently and effectively spend taxpayer dollars on transportation projects. It was a huge bill that affected every single area of the state. Speaker Straus knew I was interested in transportation legislation but, when he gave me the bill, he knew I had to be able to work it from its infancy and pass it not only out of the House but ensure I had enough support to pass it out of the Senate too. It's a lot of work that many weren't willing to do. I jumped in and worked with the Speaker and other House colleagues to advance the legislation. That September, Governor Greg Abbott signed the bill into law.

Staying Focused on the Goal

Believe it or not, I learned a lot about the political process from across the aisle. When I made my way around to 149 state representatives during my first session in the House, I met a longtime Democrat from El Paso, Joe Pickett. Joe had been representing El Paso for eighteen years when I met him in his office, entering the House in the same class as my predecessor, Burt Solomons. There wasn't anything particularly noteworthy about our meeting, but I must have made an impression as a freshman Republican going to meet with a Democrat.

Joe was chairman of the Homeland Security & Public Safety committee, and not long after our meeting, I was assigned to the committee. Joe told me later that he had asked the Speaker if I could be put on his committee. It was a great committee. We dealt with anything related to public safety. It was because of my meeting with him that Joe said, "I want that guy on my team." It carried into my second session when Joe was chairman of the Transportation committee. I wanted to be on transportation. Joe put in a good word for me, and I ended up on that committee too.

Over time I developed an incredible personal relationship with Joe. Transportation was something that wasn't very partisan, so we could work on things everybody could agree on. In Texas, we meet only for 140 days, every other year, so there are a lot more bills filed than can ever be considered and more bills referred to committees than could ever receive a hearing. The Transportation committee would meet every Thursday during the session, and I would meet Joe in his office at 8 a.m. to go through the bills that had been referred to the committee and talk through which ones he wanted to put up for a hearing. That was special for a second-session guy to be asked to do that for a legislator with nearly two decades in office, and it all started because of that initial meeting where I learned his story and asked for advice on anything I might need to know.

As time went on, I continued to see the value in relationships and focusing on the process to reach the finish line. What appeared to me as being common sense in business wasn't common sense in public service. Things were just different. When you're making public policy in a political environment, you have to process and accomplish things a little differently. In a business environment, things are reasonably black and white. You have a customer in mind, a goal, and a plan to get there. Maybe you're trying to sell a widget. The more widgets you sell, the more money you make. You make all the decisions with that one goal in mind. You can't do that when you're dealing in a relationship business like public service or a lot of other things in life. Along the way, you have to not only make sure you're heading toward the right goal but you also have to make sure you're managing the people and the relationships along the way. That's why it takes so much more time and effort to accomplish things in politics than it does in business. What would be logical to me—"Hey, this is the right policy, this is what we're going to do, let's just do it"—might not be logical to any of the other 149 Representatives. So you'd go see if that representative was OK with the policy, listen to them, tweak it, and the process would go on. I think the Lord used that as a way for me to slow down, recognize there were other people just as important as I was, and realize I wasn't going to be able to get done what I wanted unless I knew how to work with those people. It forced me to be understanding, and that helped me in my relationships at home and other places as well. What the Lord was telling me was, "Look, Ron, we've gotten a lot of good things done here, but you probably plowed through some people and that maybe wasn't the best thing. I'm going to put you in a spot where the only way you're going to get to what you really want is if you figure out how to work with people."

There are some values to having processes, but a government run like a business . . . do you know what that's called? A dictatorship. It doesn't work that way. There's no doubt that the way we have to develop public policy sucks. It's hard. It's messy. But it's the very best way to do it because it ensures every voice has a chance to be heard.

Life Doesn't Have to be Controversial

My head began spinning when Speaker Straus reminded me before my first term that only one bill had to pass each session. Around the same time, someone told me that, as a House member, I had the right to go sit in on any committee hearing, even if I wasn't on the committee. Knowing the budget was handled by the Appropriations committee, I knew that's where I needed to be.

The committee met every morning at 7:30 a.m. at the capitol. The committee would sit higher up on the dais, and people testifying would sit down below. I wasn't put on the committee, but on the first day, I showed up and approached the chairman, Republican Jim Pitts. "Mr. Chairman, is it OK if I'm here today? Do you have a place for me on the dais?" He was very gracious and welcomed me with open arms. They held daily meetings for a month, and I didn't miss one. It just made sense. I might have been fifty-one, but I had a lot to learn about the state—and I was eager to learn it. Plus, I knew if I wanted to pass a bill, it was going to cost money and end up going through the budget committee anyway. I figured I better know how it worked. As I continued to show up, the chairman occasionally called on me. "Representative Simmons, I know you're not on the committee, but do you have any questions?"

Once the committee went through its main work, it would break into subgroups that covered particular areas of the budget. I picked the General Government subcommittee, which focused on the budgets of the Governor's Office, the Attorney General, and some other agencies. The reason I chose the group was that it was run by the Appropriations committee vice chairman, a Democrat from Houston, Sylvester Turner. Sylvester was a super-smart guy and a long-term Democrat who had been elected to the House in the late 1980s. As I did with all of the other representatives, I had sat down with Sylvester and learned about him and his family. It wasn't as easy to fade into the group in the subcommittees. They were held in a conference room, and agency members would stand around the outside of the conference table to answer any questions as the group went line by line through parts of the budget. So I asked if I could sit in, and Sylvester agreed. We would meet three days each week until the budget was settled where we wanted it. Sylvester included me just like I was a member of the committee, which I really appreciated. What I learned from Sylvester in that process was most of the issues weren't partisan. You could have helicoptered into the room and if you didn't know him, at least half the time you'd have sworn he was a conservative Republican. As we worked through the budget, he'd say, "That's too much money to spend" or "That's a waste of taxpayer money." Of course, we grew up thinking every Democrat will spend every dime and more. That wasn't just always true.

One day, as we were going around the table talking, I chimed in with a comment. The lady sitting beside me, who was a Republican, said, "Well, you're not on this committee, so it doesn't matter what you think." I'll never forget the look on Sylvester's face. He looked at her and said, "I am very interested in Representative Simmons's comments, so I would appreciate you not saying that." She shut up. One of the things I learned is that most of the stuff you do in life doesn't have to be controversial, just like most things in the legislature aren't partisan. If I hadn't met Sylvester Turner in his office, it would have been a different dynamic. By the time I walked into that committee room to ask if I could sit in on the subcommittee, he and I had already developed a small but meaningful relationship. He knew I wasn't a threat. Different constituencies have different ideas, and you have to be willing to work through them. It takes time and effort to get things done. Are you willing to be a workhorse? You have to decide whether you want to hold the position or you want to make the impact. That's for all things in life. Sometimes you have to decide that it's more important to make the impact than to hold on to the position.

Several of my freshman colleagues never looked at a bill during our first session. All they did was look at a scorecard from a far-right group, and however the group said to vote on a bill, that's how they voted. *Every time.* I asked one, "Why are you doing that?" "Because I don't want to have someone run against me in the primary," he told me. I wasn't going to do it. Maybe that's why I had six opponents (both Democrat and Republican) in seven years, but I still wasn't going to do it. During my second term, another dear friend decided he was going to run for Speaker. As I had done with David Simpson, I tried to talk him out of it. "You cannot win, and you're going to put your friends at a disadvantage by doing this," I told him. This time, there was nothing we could do to change the decision. When it came down to it, I and some other people told him that, even though we were conservative, we had to break from him. It was the first contested vote for Texas Speaker since 1975. In the nineteen Speaker elections in between, prospective challengers had always dropped out to avoid a contentious vote on the first day of session. There were nineteen people who voted against Straus. To this day, that group is still called "The 19." It wasn't that our friend wouldn't have done a good job as Speaker, but there was absolutely no path for victory. I believe some of The 19 (certainly not all) voted for him because they were more worried about being reelected than they were about serving. They were more concerned about getting beat in the next campaign than they were about getting things accomplished for Texas. They didn't accomplish one thing that next session. I decided if I were defeated in a primary or the general election, then I was just going to get beat. I was there to make sure I was engaged in things that were important. I was going to worry more about serving than I was about being elected. At some point in time, those don't go together.

So many people in the political world—and it happens in other walks of life too—want to have the *position* so badly they're unwilling to take the risk to have the *impact*. I saw in people smarter than me that being a politician was their whole identity, and holding on to the position that gave them that identity was their top priority. Having been through my business career, I wasn't trying to make a name for myself. I wasn't in Austin to be somebody. I was there to *do* something.

~ Chapter 13 ~
A.C.T. (Action, Consider, Takeaway)

Action

Make a decision to be a workhorse in whatever you do. Decide now or you will tend to be influenced by circumstances instead of principles.

Consider

Are you willing to go from holding on to the handle of your wagon in a particular area to becoming the pusher, or the cargo, so that you can learn from others?

Takeaway

Accomplishing anything that makes a difference or has value is hard and carries risk. Are you willing to be the workhorse to make that "thing" in your life happen?

CHAPTER 14

Victory after Despair

*A*s I stood at my desk on the floor of the state capitol on January 10, 2017, to begin my third session and officially become a member of the 85th Texas legislature, it dawned on me how quickly life in office had passed me by. I was fifty-six years old, five years removed from deciding to run, and—because I had chosen to take a stand on several issues and faced primary challenges—had five elections in five years under my belt. And yet I looked up and it was as if those five years of my life had gone by in a flash.

I've always said the final chapter of success comes when someone decides to become a difference-maker. When I walked away from the daily minutiae of Retirement Advisors of America, I did so with a sense of pride that I had made a difference. By the time RAA sold in 2019, there were probably twenty other people closely related to the firm who became multimillionaires. They worked hard and deserved it. But the basis of building that company—and a lesson for anything you do in life—was doing everything possible so everybody involved benefited too. When other people aren't benefiting, you're on a solo track. From the time I was seventeen years old, all I ever wanted was financial independence. Once I reached that, I arrived at the pivotal moment in my life. *Where are you?* I asked myself. That's when I turned my attention to serving. I knew it from the day I made the decision to run for public office and was reminded many times in those next five years that it wasn't going to be easy. There are a lot of people who don't want to take the difficult road. But nothing in life worth doing is easy.

When I made the decision to run for state representative in the 2012 election, I was a fresh face with a clean slate. There was nothing holding me back. I could make promises and didn't have to answer for any decisions of the past. When my second and third general elections came, it was an entirely different story. I had been to Austin, stood for issues, and passed legislation. My voting history was now my record. It didn't take long to realize what that meant. If someone didn't agree with a piece of legislation I authored or a vote I made, all it took was an email alert to get the opposition fired up. I went into the 2014 general election unopposed in the Republican Party and widened the margin of victory from my first election, beating my Democratic opponent with 64.3 percent of the vote. By the time the 2016 election cycle came around, I could see the political tide turning. My propensity for action at the state capitol put me in a primary race against another Republican. And while I ended up winning with 83.2 percent of the vote, primaries were always spent trying not to lose your patience to explain your record to voters. "You guys are just down there fat-catting with the lobbyists," people would say. Or they'd ask, "Why don't you get something done? You've got a majority." It was a constant battle of deciding what to address and what to ignore. The election cycle wears on you.

I knew I was putting everything I had into being a state representative. My family was sacrificing, and there was a loud, vocal minority that constantly beat against me. After getting through my second primary in three races, I won the general election again without a major contest, garnering 56.3 percent of the vote. But while it was a third straight decisive victory over the Democratic candidate in District 65, it was becoming clear a blue wave—brought on in large part by one-punch, straight-ticket voting—was beginning to tighten the margin of victory.

I really looked forward to my third session in the House. As much as you try to prepare for it, I learned that it took a couple of sessions to get fully ingrained in the legislative process. I got things done every session, but going into the third session I knew I was going to be engaged in important legislation. I knew I was going to be called on to become a decision-maker. "Making difficult decisions invites criticism," Speaker Straus said during his speech on the first day of my third session. Boy, did I learn that. In the next 140 days in session, I would help author and pass one major piece of legislation and carry two others, one for the Speaker and the other for the Governor, shaping the trajectory of my political career.

Deciding What's Important

When Governor Greg Abbott asked me to carry House Bill 1335 to establish an education savings account program for children with special needs, I didn't hesitate. Daniel was an adult by that time, and Lisa and I could always afford the best schools for him when he was growing up, but I knew there were a lot of people who didn't have those resources. I wasn't going to be in the legislature and not try to pass the bill.

In Texas, school choice isn't an issue that's a Democrat versus Republican battle. Instead, it often boils down to Democrats and rural Republicans opposing suburban Republicans. My mom and dad were both public school teachers, so I knew what I was going up against and the challenges standing for the issue could create for my political career. I decided the issue of school choice for students with special needs was more important than my being reelected. I think you have to decide that in anything you do in life. I had gotten into public service to do something, and I wasn't going to let the possibility of losing an election affect the decisions I made. So I carried the bill. I felt the backlash almost immediately. A large majority of public school teachers and administrators came out against me. My only regret was that the bill didn't even make it to the House floor for a vote. The Speaker had promised to allow the bill to go to the floor, but he didn't. In the end, he had members who knew it would be hard to vote against children with special needs; they didn't want to have a vote, because public school teachers in their districts didn't want any school choice bills passed and they didn't want to face the repercussions. I knew carrying the bill was risky. In my district, the largest employer was the public school system. I filed HB 1335 less than three weeks into my third session, and three months later the bill was dead, left pending in the Public Education committee.

It wasn't long after my school choice bill was handed off to the committee that I met with the Speaker's chief of staff and explained an idea for a bill that I thought would be an answer to what I saw as an impending disaster across Texas. A debate was building across the state and the nation regarding transgender people using bathrooms and locker rooms other than those of their biological gender. Across Texas's 254 counties, cities and school districts were setting different rules. I thought the answer to the issue was to prohibit political subdivisions (school districts, counties, cities, and so forth) of the state from setting rules or policies related to this issue but that the debate should rightly be held at the statehouse by the elected members of the legislature, and whatever policy was implemented through law would be the same statewide. The chief of staff consulted with Speaker Straus and encouraged me to file the bill.

Again, the bill wasn't a policy declaration on what was right or wrong. It was only meant to stop the influx of city-by-city rules until the state could come up with a uniform policy. I had eighty colleagues coauthor the bill, giving me an 80 out of 150 majority. But despite asking me to file and work the bill, the Speaker didn't let the bill get to the House floor. He decided it wasn't worth the fight with the Democrats. I had been thrown under the bus. That was a valuable lesson—just when you think you have your red wagon handle leading the charge and in control, something is going to come up and remind you that you don't have control.

In between the two bills I helped carry for the Governor and the Speaker, I authored House Bill 25 to eliminate one-punch, straight-ticket voting. The previous fall I had seen my election tighten to its smallest margin. I had still won by more than twelve points, but my races were getting closer and closer to the Democratic candidate, even when they weren't spending very much to campaign. I knew whether I continued to run for office or if I passed the torch to another Republican candidate, the race could get close. But it wasn't just about my district or me. I knew if we left straight-ticket voting in place that Texas was going to be worse off. Having constituents go into the ballot box and blindly vote all "R" or all "D" without looking down the ballot was going to end up with unqualified elected officials. Throughout the spring of 2017, I worked the bill. It eventually passed out of the House on May 6, 2017, with a vote of 88–57. If the bill passed the Senate, it would become effective three months later, well ahead of the 2018 general election.

But as I learned many times and was reminded again ten days later—not all roads in life are straight. When the bill reached the Senate floor, it was quickly met with an amendment. *"In SECTION 2 of the bill, in added Section 31.012 (b-1), Election Code, strike 'September 1, 2017' and substitute 'September 1, 2020.'"* Instead of becoming effective that fall, if passed, the bill wouldn't take effect until *after* the next election. Even as my races were getting closer, I still thought I could win if I ran a fourth time. Plus, I believed in the elimination of one-punch, straight-ticket voting and in people making decisions based on policy instead of party. Despite the delay and the potential repercussions, I continued to work the bill. It eventually passed out of the Senate and was signed by Governor Abbott on June 1, 2017, with an effective date of September 1, 2020. It was easily the most impactful bill I authored and passed. This legislation will affect elections in Texas for decades to come, and I believe for the better.

As my third session wound down, I faced a stern realization as I headed home from Austin. There I was, considered a senior member of the House with a good reputation, and even though I had successfully completed difficult bills before and knew my road in that 140-day session would be difficult, I was hit by things out of my control. Sometimes in life, you're engaged in something and it's not about you. You may be a part of it, but it's not about you. You wonder, *Why did this happen?* We're not the star player in everything in life the way we sometimes think we are (or wish we were). The Lord has had to remind me of that on more than one occasion, and he seems to do it swiftly and directly. That reminder was about to come.

Back on the Campaign Trail

On July 3, 1863, the Confederate Army of Northern Virginia, composed of nearly fifteen thousand soldiers, pushed along Cemetery Ridge in Gettysburg, Pennsylvania, in what would become known as Pickett's Charge. For three-quarters of a mile, the soldiers pressed on, uphill and exposed against the Union soldiers.

The Confederate soldiers had assembled and made their assault on the Union Army at the order of General Robert E. Lee, who was coming off a string of successes, including just two months earlier in the Battle of Chancellorsville. When Lee hopped on his famous horse, Traveller, that morning and rode along Cemetery Ridge to meet with his generals, he was confident. "General, I have been a soldier all my life," General James Longstreet told Lee before Pickett's Charge. "I have been with soldiers engaged in fights by couples, by squads, companies, regiments, divisions, and armies, and should know, as well as anyone, what soldiers can do. It is my opinion that no 15,000 men ever arranged for battle can take that position." Even when General Longstreet voiced his concern, Lee never entertained changing his plans or altering his approach. He was wrapped up in winning and emboldened by his success. Lee commanded the men to push up the hill.

By that afternoon, Lee's Confederate Army had suffered more than six thousand casualties. The charge became the turning point in the Civil War and the end of the Battle of Gettysburg. When Lee saw Longstreet later, he conceded, "It's all my fault. I thought my men were invincible." Lee had gotten so used to winning the battles and was such a smart commander that he felt invincible. That's where leaders can find themselves in trouble. When you've had a run of successes, you can feel like your intuition is always right. Because it *has* been right. But when you get comfortable, you quit going through the checks and balances. That's what Lee did. He felt he had a stronger army than the North. He didn't know for sure, but he felt that way and pushed his people ahead into harm's way.

The final year of my political career wasn't quite as dire. But when I looked back later, I wondered if I had counted on the past to carry me to a fourth term. The warning signs were there. Before the *Titanic* sank in 1912, the crew had been told about potential icebergs. They didn't realize that while they only saw a small tip, most of the iceberg was underwater. Sometimes, when trouble starts to put its head up, and you think it isn't a big deal, it could be a big deal. You need to investigate. When I decided to run for state representative for the fourth time, the attacks began almost immediately. "Let's flush Ron down the toilet," my new opponent told her supporters. I was painted as "Bathroom Bill Ron" to the Democrats. She repeatedly hit me with negative campaigns. "Tax money for private schools" and "voter suppression." I knew taking a stand and carrying bills I believed in would leave me exposed to criticism, but from the time I was first elected, I had always told myself that I'd rather get voted out of office than not stand for the things I believed in and make a difference. Now I was facing that very battle.

To complicate matters, after I made the decision to run for a fourth term in the fall of 2017, I learned I was going to have a Republican primary opponent for the third time. Even worse, the guy was running because he had the same last name as me. When voters went to voting booths the next spring for the primary, they would choose between Kevin Simmons and Ron Simmons. *Oh, my*, I thought, *I have to make sure people know who I am.* Sure, I had been in the House for three sessions, but I knew people were easily confused when it came to politicians. They might know the name Simmons, but they might not know the difference between Kevin and Ron. In state representative races in Texas, primary costs run into the hundreds of thousands of dollars. And while I raised money and campaigned for the Republican primary, my Democratic opponent didn't have a primary—so she spent all her time hitting me during *my* primary. I had two opponents working against me. Since I had this other Simmons against me, I had to launch a big campaign and make sure the "Ron" on my signs was bigger than the "Simmons." Leading up to the March 2018 primary, I knocked on doors and attended chicken dinners. As the primary neared, the Republican Party held a ballot draw to determine the order on the ballot for the races. When they reached the District 65 race, both Kevin and I jumped up to draw out of the hat. The person holding the hat wasn't sure what to do. "Who gets to draw the number?" they asked. Being the incumbent, I probably could have drawn, but I decided I was going to be the bigger person. "You know what, Kevin," I said, "you go ahead and draw." I didn't know if he would draw one or two, but I wasn't going to put up a fight. Luckily, he drew a two. I would be listed first on the primary ballot. We spent a lot of money on the race and worked hard. When the primary arrived on March 6, 2018, it paid off. My opponent ended up not being a good candidate, and I won easily with 83.3 percent of the vote.

That same day, Democrat Robert Frances "Beto" O'Rourke won the primary for the US Senate, pitting him against Republican Ted Cruz in the 2018 general election. There wasn't much time to start my campaign for the fall. Not only did my Democratic opponent have extra time, but she also now had the Beto Effect and one-punch voting behind her too. I learned in the primary that nothing is assured. The general election would only hammer that lesson home. While my opponent launched a negative advertising campaign, my longtime consultant advised against that same tactic, and I agreed. We ran a poll to test her name recognition. She had finished third in a three-horse mayoral race in Carrollton, a city of about one hundred thousand where she and I both lived, but she had a simple name and had pretty good name recognition; at least, people thought they knew who she was. Our theory was that if we fired back against her insults, we'd only increase her name recognition. Therefore, I should just ignore her. Looking back, it was a huge mistake. I don't put the blame on my consultant. I was, by this time, experienced in politics so I could have easily overridden his suggestion. We ended up disregarding her and stayed focused on, "Here's what Ron has done." She was hitting me the whole time. I campaigned as if it were a normal election.

I talked to as many constituents as I could and arrived at the polls early on November 6, 2018, to meet as many voters as I could. By the end of the day, I had made my way to all sixteen polling locations in District 65. When the call came in from the chairperson of the Denton County Republican Party, I was down 200 votes. I still remembered what my consultant had told me on Election Day of my first campaign: it was hard to come back from an early deficit. I skipped the Republican Party campaign event and headed home to watch the results. By the end of the night, Cruz had defeated O'Rourke by 214,921 votes—a mere 2.6 percentage points—but he lost in most suburban areas like mine. It was ironic. The teachers weren't in my favor—all of the local teacher groups went against me—and thousands of people went to the polls and participated in one-punch voting to vote for O'Rourke and all the Democrats down the ballot. I didn't have enough to overcome the Beto Effect. I lost by 1,358 votes.

Maybe we should have done more of a comparison between myself and my Democratic opponent. We probably would have been more effective had we drawn the differences between us so that people would make a real choice. Maybe we were too confident. But I didn't really blame anybody. At the end of the day, people didn't pay attention. None of that probably even mattered. Voters just went into the booth and punched the Democratic ticket to cast their vote for Beto.

Redefining Life's Victories

As I drove my Silverado toward the North Carolina mountains a few weeks after my loss, I couldn't help but second-guess the events of the previous months. I thought about the bills I authored and helped carry in my final session. I thought about the campaign. *What could I have done differently?* I wondered.

But as the miles ticked up on my odometer, I came to a realization. Maybe measuring victory wasn't as simple as counting votes. Sometimes in life, it's easy to see what victory looks like—it's black and white. But in many areas of life, if you have a predetermined view of exactly how victory is supposed to look and feel, you may end up disappointed. I made my trek to the mountains to find out why I was so disappointed about losing the election. *How could it mean so much to me?* What I found was that I had measured victory by whether I was elected to a fourth term. The truth about life is we need to adapt and change our definition of victory. While we may feel defeated, we may not see the entire picture. God might only be revealing it to us as we go along. Lisa and I have made mistakes with that. Sometimes we don't realize that we're living in a victorious situation until we look back and see it that way later. At the moment, it wasn't exactly how we thought it should be in our finite, linear minds. Sometimes when things are the darkest is when God is most at work. At any point in your life where you reach a fork in the road and something didn't go the way you thought it should or wanted, you have to be open and willing to accept another definition of victory. There are some neat things that can come out of disappointment and heartbreak, where God will give you perspective and also remind you of some of the good things that occurred. It was following my loss that God showed me he was, and still is, in the blessing business.

Not long after I was asked by the new Speaker and Governor Abbott to serve as chairman of the Texas Mutual Insurance Company, I went to Austin to thank some people for their past support. While I was there, I met up for cocktails with a friend, Kevin Roberts, who was CEO of the largest state-based think tank in the country, the Texas Public Policy Foundation. As a conservative think tank, they had played a big role in trying to help me get the school choice legislation done. "Ron, I'd like for you to come help us out," he said. I didn't want to lobby, and I wasn't interested in doing anything full time. "What does that mean?" I asked. "We really want to do some work on welfare reform," he told me. He asked me to come on as an

outside consultant and help think about ways to work with the legislature better and craft policy around welfare reform.

I said it before, but I've always felt like but for the grace of God,
there go I. I don't know why my life turned out the way it did as a
boy raised by two teachers from Arkansas in a lower-middle-class
family. There were so many fork-in-the-road moments in my life
where I could have gone down another path that kept me stuck in my
situation. I don't know why I ended up where I did. But it gives me
a soft spot for people who are in a disadvantaged situation but want
to get out of it. There are so many people who are just looking for an
opportunity. It's always been my belief that 98 percent of the people
who are on government assistance would prefer not to be if they
could figure out how to get off it and still thrive. The way our system
works today is that people are penalized when they take a job or get a
promotion—their government benefits are cut so much that they're
better off not taking that job or earning that promotion. Those are
called *welfare cliffs*. You work your way up to a certain amount and
then lose basically everything. This was another blessing that the
Lord sent my way, presenting me the opportunity to be engaged in
policy and have an effect on policy without being elected. I didn't
have to be in public office to influence public policy. I joined the
think tank and started working to promote a stair-step system so
that, as someone who is on government assistance becomes more
independent, their personal income plus their government assistance never is less than what government assistance would have been
if they hadn't worked.

As I began working on the other side and meeting with former
colleagues back in Austin, I was reminded of the lessons I had
learned earlier in my career. The fact that I went and met with all
those members, the fact that we "disagreed agreeably" on policy
issues, and the fact that people saw me as a serious policy person
meant that when I stepped to the other side, those members paid

attention. Because of that, I've been able to work behind the scenes where people will never know, moving the ball on legislation and issues I thought were interesting and important—and I didn't have to be the person pushing the button (or pulling the wagon). Even in defeat, God showed me a path that felt victorious.

The opportunities that came my way after what I thought was a devastating loss were phenomenal. And yet, had anyone asked me about those opportunities before I lost my election for a fourth term as state representative, I wouldn't have seen them as remotely beneficial. They weren't my definition of victory. I had to have the willingness to take the next uncomfortable step, because a lot of times, if it doesn't look like victory is coming in the way you expect it, you'll stop, try to turn, and go in a different direction. You must have faith that gives you the ability to take the next uncomfortable step, even though things don't look exactly like you thought they would or should. You have to have the courage to find victory after despair.

~ Chapter 14 ~
A.C.T. (Action, Consider, Takeaway)

Action

Life throws us curveballs. Make a list of the curveballs in your life, the twists and turns that have hit when you least expected them.

Consider

How much personal risk are you willing to take for what you know to be the greater good? It's a serious question that requires serious thought. Take the time to think on this and be brutally honest with yourself.

Takeaway

Victory often occurs after despair if we allow it to happen. Don't miss your next blessing by focusing too much on your most recent disappointment.

CHAPTER 15

Dreams of a Better Tomorrow

*H*ave you ever gone for a walk and watched a child play in his or her red wagon? They're so hopeful. Their entire life is ahead of them, and the worst thing they have to worry about is getting a scrape on their knee. They haven't a care in the world.

When I think back to those times, I'm reminded of the 1960s hit television series *The Andy Griffith Show* and the quaint, laid-back fictitious Mayberry, North Carolina. The one-stoplight town may have been imaginary, but when Sheriff Andy Taylor went fishing or played guitar, the life portrayed on the black-and-white screen in our living rooms felt so real and so simple.

There is one specific episode where Andy and his best friend and deputy, Barney Fife, are sitting on Andy's porch one evening after dinner and relaxing when a conversation begins along the lines of, "We should go to town and get a bottle of pop," Andy says. Barney repeats him, "Yeah, we should go to town and get a bottle of pop." Andy waits a moment and chimes back in, "Do you want to go to town and get a bottle of pop?" Barney responds, "A bottle of pop would sure be good. Maybe we should go to town and get a bottle of pop." This entire exchange is humorous, of course, but the easygoing nature they have in this scene reminded me of a simpler time where life wasn't so overcomplicated.

Where are you now? Has life turned out exactly the way you thought it would when you were younger? Probably not because it's life! Life is crazy. It happens like that. "When you're young you think you will always be," Griffith said. "As you become more fragile, you reflect and you realize how much comfort can come from the past." Maybe your life hasn't gone exactly as you planned. So what? With a plan and some direction, it's possible to get back to that simplicity.

I want people like you to take the lead in your own life and determine the path you want to take, the load you want to carry, and the people you want to bring with you on the journey. When you aren't intentional about your life, you are at the whim of everything around you—other people, circumstances, your upbringing, and the opportunities that pass you by. So it should come as no surprise when you find yourself plodding forward and unable to get out of your rut. Life will never go as planned, but that doesn't mean you shouldn't have a plan. The people you meet in life who seem to always have it together not only have a plan but also constantly revise that plan to make it better and keep them on the right track. The question you must consider: Do you believe you are made for something more? It doesn't matter where you came from. If I can do it, so can you. What matters is whether or not you are willing to push forward and move off into the next phase of your adventure.

There's no reason I should have been successful. I was a kid from small-town Arkansas whose mom and dad were public school teachers. My parents divorced when I was seventeen, I moved out to live on my own, and it took me ten years to earn my college degree. There was nothing special about me that said I should have been able to be successful, nothing that pointed to my being involved in the leadership of the second-largest state in America. In America, those things happen, but there's no real reason. I believe the Lord has had an outsized impact on all of it, but, as I look back on my life, I also believe there were wagon pushers and pullers in my life, people who were put in my life who were willing to be a puller or a pusher and show me how to do those things. Sometimes in my marriage, Lisa has had to be the puller. I had no idea what to do with our fifteen-year-old daughter! (Sometimes, you get worn out and you gotta ride.) Multiple times, Lisa has been the spiritual giant in our family, not so much with her words but with her actions of daily prayer, devotional time, and Bible study. I have watched her do this day in, day out for forty-one years, and I know her relationship with Christ has carried us through times when my faith was less than it should have been.

When I was younger, I had one vision: financial independence. For seventeen years, I saw the struggles of my family and I was determined not to fall into mediocrity. That was my driving force. It didn't matter how I got there. I didn't have a passion for the investment business. I just wanted to be able to get there—wherever "there" was. I believe there are a lot of people just like me out there, people who, in light of their family situations or their upbringing, want to break free. They're asking, "How do I get on a different path?" Maybe that person is you. As I look back, there was a road map I followed, and along the way there were pushers and pullers who were important to me. Sometimes you have to follow your gut and take the steps you believe in your heart are the right ones to take. Whether it was moving away from the small town we grew up in, walking away from business to spend time with my family, or risking political clout for what I believed in, I had to make decisions along the way. A wagon has only one handle. At the end of the day, somebody has to make the decision. The person holding the handle determines the direction and the first step. You can change direction at any time. You are in control of your life. But sometimes you have to lead—you have to decide.

Where are you in life right now? This could refer to your age, career, opportunities, or goals. What are they? Do you know? Here's what I know: I'm not sure where you find yourself now, but you can decide right now to change direction. Start by thinking about these questions:

Where are you stuck? It happens to the best of us. We lose momentum. We get stuck in a rut. We run out of steam. You feel out of control of your own life and have no idea when or if you'll be able to move forward. If you want to end up at the finish line, you've got to take stock of where you are stuck and where you can grow. What factors are holding you back?

Where do you want to go from here? You can't get any momentum because you aren't sure where you're going; every direction seems plausible, so life is a series of fits and starts. You live at the whim of others. Wherever circumstances go, that's where you follow. If you haven't figured out the finish line, now's the time. Consider where you are now, where you are proficient, and where you'd like to end up. You'll never know if you are on the right track if you don't have a destination in mind.

What is stopping you? There are many things that can hold you back, but you have to do some investigation to find out what they are. Are the things holding you back self-inflicted or caused by others? Is your history a hindrance? Are you getting in your own way? When you push futilely forward, but the view never changes, you get worn out from trying. You have to think about what is causing friction before you can move forward.

Who's pulling your wagon? It's worthwhile to answer this question and see if you are actually in charge of the direction of your own life. Are you leading or drifting? Are you taking the easy road or pulling into a more difficult path? Are you following the crowd or charting your own course? Remember that sometimes life's journey calls for us to get inside the wagon.

Growth can't happen if you are stuck in a rut. When you work to take charge of your life, there's another way. Instead of feeling stuck, you feel liberated. Where you once felt directionless, you now clearly see the way forward. Instead of feeling frustrated, you feel empowered. While you used to feel overloaded, suddenly you feel the wrong burdens falling away and renewed strength to carry the right load. And where you used to feel stalled, you now feel energized as success builds on success, and the road ahead is free and clear.

One of life's biggest challenges is that people can't visualize themselves charting a new path or aiming for a different destination. For most people, the top of the mountain doesn't just appear out of nowhere. Getting there is a process of putting one foot in front of the other over time. If someone would have told me when we started our investment business that when we got to the end of it we'd be in all fifty states with $3 billion under management, I wouldn't have believed it. Even if you ask me today what it looked like, it didn't just happen. It was one phone call and one pilot visit at a time. That's all it was. There wasn't an epiphany. It wasn't just *Boom!* In early 2019, with Retirement Advisors of America's EBITDA (earnings before interest, taxes, depreciation, and amortization) growing, and what looked to be a significant increase in the value of firms like ours to buyers, I raised a question during a board meeting. "We ought to see what people would pay for us," I said. While the board wasn't that interested in selling, one member spoke up: "But if somebody will meet our number . . ."

Five months later, RAA had five offers over that number. *Man, that is a lot of money*, I would think to myself. There is no question that's true, but until I left RAA, I never really thought in those terms because when we started, we began with no clients and added one retired pilot at a time. That's just how the business grew. We stayed in the daily grind and kept on talking to pilots who were getting ready to retire. We didn't get off the path here or there. We eyed our destination and pushed toward it.

When I was done, I faced the burning question of life: *What's next?* That "what's next" comes in all areas of our lives.

What's next in my career?

What's next in my faith?

What's next in my family?

It's not just a "what's next?" in one area; it's everything. What's next for you? Making that decision can be terrifying. I know! Throughout my life, I always approached decisions with the mindset that if everything went to hell in a handbasket, I could start over, rebuild, and do it again. Maybe that was naive, but I always believed in my mind that making a decision wasn't the end of the world. There's a saying that Lisa taught me: *Everything is fixable.* There's almost nothing in life—other than death—that is so devastating that it's the end of your entire existence on this earth. I remember Lisa's concerned response when I went into business on my own. "What do you mean you're leaving that company and starting your own?" she said. Making a decision like that might have been scary, but I believed it was going to work. There's no question that people run from fear. You have to decide what's important to you and say to yourself, *What path do I have to take to accomplish it?* I tell people all the time, and it's the truth: if the Lord called me home today, I would miss my family, but I would think, *Man, what a life I have lived*. I have not left anything on the table. Could I have made some better choices? No question. I've made plenty of mistakes. But I have always tried to get to the maximum, whatever that happened to be.

Not long after we were married, Lisa and I wrote down some goals, folded them up, and put them in the desk inside the mobile home we lived in at the time. I've always been a goal-setter, but I never really thought about the goals after we stashed them inside the desk. A few years later, as we cleaned out the desk drawer, we came across the sheet of paper and unfolded it. *We had met every one of them*. I can't even remember what all of them were; they weren't necessarily big. I do remember one of them was to get a new washing machine. We had never talked about them, but they were etched in our minds. No matter what, they were subconsciously there. It's so important to write things down. I promise you there's a little something in the back of your head going, *Don't you remember?* It may be pushed back, but it's there.

Goals and dreams are what make our wagons worth pulling and pushing. You'll end up nowhere if you don't know where you're going. You can do all the right things, but if you don't have a goal or a plan, then where are you going? You end up doing the best you can, but no better. If you don't have a vision of the finish line or what the horizon might look like, you won't get where you want. You need a vision of what success looks like—for *you*. What success looks like for you might be very different from what it looks like for me. The decisions you make will determine your path forward. Growth happens only when you push on, pull forward, and strive for the distant horizon.

So grab the handle and take the next uncomfortable step.

~ Chapter 15 ~
A.C.T. (Action, Consider, Takeaway)

Action

Write down a plan for those things that are important
in your life. They don't have to be grandiose—just get
started. Don't put this off. Do it, and please do it now! It
will change your life; that is a promise!

Consider

Spend some time thinking on *why* things are important
that you deem important. What makes them a priority for
you? Maybe some of them are *not* so important after all?

Takeaway

It is OK to dream, but a dream without a plan is just a
wish. Make a plan!

The "C" Word

*B*ook projects are by nature a long process, often taking months or even years to complete and publish. This book has been no different. While I began compiling my thoughts for this book years ago, we started our work in earnest in very early 2021, with the world still gripped in a pandemic and a couple of months after a very controversial presidential election in the United States.

Over these last few years, we have witnessed a lot of changes in our country and experienced quite a few changes in our family as well. We welcomed a new grandchild into the world and we saw one of our children and family move three hundred miles away for a better job opportunity. However, nothing we witnessed or experienced prepared us for the double-barreled news we would receive in the spring of 2022.

Lisa and I were married on March 15, 1980, the Ides of March. While we certainly did not receive the fate of Julius Caesar, we will never forget our forty-second wedding anniversary in 2022. Like most women, Lisa goes for an annual checkup with her gynecologist and March 2022 was no different. Part of the exam included a mammogram. When I asked how her checkup went, she said, "Oh, it was fine. They said they wanted to do another mammogram; they saw some denseness. I don't know why they want to do this. I have always been told I have dense breast tissue." I didn't think any more about it, and I don't think she did either. The follow-up mammogram/sonogram was scheduled for a week later on March 22. We went on with our lives, celebrated our forty-second wedding anniversary on March 15 by having dinner with some longtime friends, and enjoyed having our three grandsons (who had moved away the previous year) spend a few days with us during their spring break from school.

Tuesday, March 22, arrived and again we were not concerned about the second mammogram, convinced that it was simply an overly cautious medical professional seeing "dense tissue" and nothing else. I had some public policy work to do in Austin, so I left that evening for meetings the next day. If memory serves, Lisa received the call from her doctor the next day with the news. There was a small tumor mass in her right breast, and a biopsy would be required—quickly—to see if it was malignant cancer. Lisa called me immediately in Austin late Wednesday. As you can imagine, it was quite the emotional call, but in our shock, we still held out hope it would simply be a benign mass and life would go on.

Six days later a biopsy was performed and a few days later a phone call came: "Lisa, you have a malignant tumor, and you need to contact a breast cancer surgeon."

Wait a minute—what was happening? We went into a small spiral but quickly rebounded, and Lisa started her serious journey of learning all she could about this disease and the various ways it could be successfully treated. Her experience as a teacher and a lifelong love of learning really came into play during this time.

As providence would have it, Lisa had just hung up the phone with a friend who is a doctor at Baylor Hospital in Dallas minutes before the doctor called with the biopsy results. When he said, "You need to find a breast surgeon," she immediately called her friend back and asked who she would recommend. She said without hesitation, "Dr. Michael Grant." While it was a relief to have such a strong recommendation, Lisa wanted to ask other friends who she knew had recently experienced breast cancer. She talked to three different people within forty-eight hours and all of them recommended the same surgeon: Dr. Grant.

While the consistency of hearing Dr. Grant's name was a comfort, the fear of the unknown, as well as what we knew from other friends who had gone through similar diagnoses, was definitely bubbling to the top. Every story we had ever heard—the good, the bad, and the ugly—came to mind, from people we knew who had fought valiantly using every medical treatment available, to those who had fought just as hard and, sadly, lost the battle. Which would Lisa be?

Our first meeting with Dr. Grant was surreal. He is a professing Christian with a gentle manner, so he did his best to put us at ease. The artwork he had on the wall behind him was a painting with Jesus looking over the shoulder of the surgeon. Again, comforting, but fear is a powerful force. Thankfully, we had the presence of mind to record the meeting. There's no way either of us could have remembered all that he said. Lisa said it reminded her of the game she and Allie Beth used to play called "Would You Rather?" In that game you give two choices to your opponent, both of which are either terrible, scary, or gross, and they *have* to choose one. When Dr. Grant told Lisa she would have to choose between a lumpectomy plus radiation and possibly chemotherapy, or a mastectomy with or without reconstruction, she felt she had just been challenged with the worst game of "Would You Rather?" ever.

Again, God goes before. A couple of years before, Lisa had reconnected with an old friend, Erin Prendergast. Erin's husband, Jeff, and I had worked together twenty years ago. Since Jeff left our company, we had lost touch, so Lisa was excited to see Erin on Facebook. The unusual part was that Lisa had seen Erin comment on a mutual friend's Facebook page. Erin had no other friends in common with Lisa and the other woman, so it seemed odd.

Fast-forward two years. I had gone to play golf alone. I told the golf pro that if there was anyone who wanted to play, I was happy to join them. The pro suggested another solo golfer and began to introduce us. No introduction was needed—it was Jeff Prendergast, Erin's husband and my former colleague. How's that for timing? We enjoyed a round of golf and set up a date for dinner with our wives.

At the dinner, we didn't talk about Lisa's new diagnosis since we were just getting reacquainted, but Erin talked about her recent retirement from nursing. After Lisa's biopsy, she decided to call Erin just to see if she could give her advice on care and recovery. Even though the doctors had given us instructions, Lisa felt talking to a friend might be a little more comforting. When she told Erin about her diagnosis, Erin said, "Lisa, this is what I've spent the last seventeen years doing. I was a cancer navigator. I took people from diagnosis through every step of their journey toward health."

For some reason during our dinner conversation a few nights before, the exact kind of nurse Erin was hadn't come up. Erin's number was definitely on speed dial after that! God so graciously reconnected Lisa and Erin well in advance of our knowing why.

Still, the decision on which choice to make—lumpectomy and radiation or mastectomy and reconstruction—was hanging over us. I could not, no matter how badly I would have liked, have made this decision for Lisa. She knew that I respected her decision no matter what. Her first instinct was to just "take it off"—have the mastectomy and be done with it. It was Erin's words of wisdom that gave Lisa the peace of mind she needed. Erin said, "That's almost always the first instinct and that may be the way to go, but you don't have to make that decision right now." Basically, "slow your roll." Even though the doctor had essentially told us the same thing, hearing Erin say it gave Lisa (and me) courage not to make a panicked decision. A few days later, Lisa made the decision to do the lumpectomy and radiation. The relief that we both felt after making that decision, even though we still didn't know all of the variables, was the first moment of clarity since this had begun.

If it were only as simple as making the decision to have the lumpectomy, that would have been sweet. However, in our lives, as I'm sure in most people's, there are many, many moving parts. Lisa is a songwriter. She writes mostly Christian, worship, and some country music. She had been planning a songwriting retreat for August of that year.

Lisa is also a researcher. She has never been willing to just take the first answer, no matter how well-intentioned, well-trained, or even confident someone was. When our son Daniel was first diagnosed with PDD-NOS at age five and the doctors gave Lisa a list of the things we shouldn't expect him to accomplish, she basically said, "Watch me." This diagnosis was no different. Once the initial shock subsided, she set out to see what she could do naturally. It just so happened that a woman in our Bible fellowship class at church came up to Lisa one Sunday about a month after her lumpectomy and told her about a friend who followed Chris Wark, a man who had beaten cancer almost 100 percent naturally. Lisa jumped into the information wholeheartedly and told me she was going to begin following his protocol. She was not saying she wasn't also going to follow the advice of her physician, but she would do everything in her power to give her body the best chance to fight naturally.

I was skeptical. This was a radical change from the way we normally ate. It was completely vegan. As Chris says, "no meat, no wheat, no sweets, and nothing from a teat." Lisa decided to try it for ninety days. This would take her through her radiation and the end of summer. It worked wonders. The benefits to her health have been multifold. Not only did she lose weight she had struggled to lose for years, but she felt better and sailed through radiation treatments. The radiologist was astonished. He had told her that she would have side effects including burning (like a sunburn), itching, and possibly swelling. She had none of those. I firmly believe the fact that she had taken control of this part of her health made a difference not only mentally but physically.

Who Has the Wagon Handle?

Something we didn't know at the time was how Lisa's decision to change her lifestyle and eating habits would affect my health as well—and how critically important that would be.

Two weeks after Lisa finished her radiation, I was diagnosed with prostate cancer.

It was the summer of 2021 when I had lunch with my friend, Bart, after not seeing each other for a couple of months, that I noticed his significant weight loss. As someone who has had periodic weight struggles for the past twenty-five years, I was obviously impressed and also curious how he lost the weight, so I asked him. Bart explained that he had started seeing a new primary care doctor, Dr. Shaun Murphy, who also had a nutritionist on staff, and they had developed an eating program that had worked for him. As many of you know, the older you get, the less effect exercise has on weight loss. In my opinion, after age forty weight loss is about 75 percent nutrition and 25 percent exercise, and a lot of research tends to back that up. Of course we all should regularly exercise, and its importance increases as we age. I decided I would get an appointment with Bart's doctor and see if something could work for me.

Dr. Murphy and his nutritionist gave me an eating plan to follow and also scheduled blood work. Most of my labs were good, but my cholesterol was high and Dr. Murphy prescribed a statin. He also mentioned that my prostate-specific antigen (PSA) was slightly elevated and suggested I see a urologist. He referred me to Dr. Joseph Scales to set up an appointment. My PSA had fluctuated in the past, so I was not worried and in no hurry to see the urologist. Any man who has gone to see a urologist knows what I mean when I say it is *not* something to look forward to!

I saw Dr. Scales in early 2022. His prostate exam found no abnormalities and he wanted to do another PSA test. To my pleasure and the doctor's surprise, my PSA had declined from the previous test. It was still a little above normal, so Dr. Scales said I should have it checked again in ninety days. By spring, it had gone back up. We were in the middle of Lisa's cancer diagnosis and deciding on a treatment plan, so I told the doctor I did not want to do anything until Lisa was on the other side of surgery and radiation. He assured me that even if there was something wrong with my prostate, it would be slow-growing so waiting would not be a problem. He did, however, convince me to have an MRI so we could better know if there was a tumor. Even the MRI was not a rush, so we scheduled it for July 8. This would be long after Lisa's surgery in May and also would allow us to spend some time in our happy place—the mountains of western North Carolina.

Based on the information I knew at the time, I was not concerned about my overall health other than wanting to lose some weight—which I was working on. I felt confident being in control of my wagon, and by gosh we were moving ahead as normal. We got to the mountains just after Memorial Day. I enjoyed three days of golf with my friend John Maxwell and about twenty other men and women at a special event John hosts every summer to raise money for Equip Leadership. This is always a special time where we rekindle friendships, eat good food, laugh a lot, and experience something unique that we did not expect. This year was no different. We were treated to playing one of the finest (and probably most exclusive) nine-hole golf courses in the country, Headwaters. It is a Tom Fazio design, and we not only played the course but were treated to lunch and a Q&A with Tom Fazio himself! He is one of world's premier course designers, so it was a fantastic surprise.

Also during this time of recovery for Lisa and relaxation for us both, our oldest son and I played in the member-guest tournament at our golf club in North Carolina, our two oldest grandsons visited for a week, and our daughter and her family came up for a few days. June was a great month of rejuvenation and relaxation for the Simmons family. We knew we needed it, but we were soon to learn just how important it is to value those happy times with the ones you love the most.

Lisa had her surgery in early May and scheduled her radiation treatments to begin in early July. I scheduled my MRI for July 8 so we flew home on July 4. We were happy and knew we were blessed to be able to have the time away in June but we were also a little anxious, not for me but for Lisa, as we again had to climb into our red wagon and be someone else's cargo going down a road we had never taken: Lisa's radiation.

The Internet is a great tool, but when you are researching medical issues you will find the good and the bad. It allows you to know what to possibly expect, but it also can stir up unnecessary fears, and believe me, Lisa and I both had those. I never spoke of my concerns about Lisa's situation to her; my job was to listen to anything she had to say, cry with her, be silent with her, pray for her, but most of all encourage her and love her. That is what we did during her radiation. I joined her almost every day of the twenty days she went for radiation. Even though it was a twenty-minute appointment at most and I had to stay in the waiting room, I wanted to be there for her. I think that meant something to her and it certainly meant something to me to make sure—through sickness and health—I was physically and emotionally present for the love of my life.

The one day that I could not go to her radiation appointment was July 8, the date of my MRI. When we left the house that morning, I remember us both laughing and saying, "Is this the future—everything revolving around doctors' appointments?" Of course we didn't think so, but deep inside we were both wondering what the future would hold and also wondering, *Where is God in all this?* It seemed like our red wagon was heading into the abyss, and not only did we not know how to grab the handle this time; we were questioning who to trust to steer us through.

The MRI I had was a relatively new and special type that, if needed, could be used again in surgery as a specific guide for the doctor to better know where the problem was, if there was one, and treat that area specifically. The appointment was uneventful. A radiologist would look at the images and send his report to my urologist, Dr. Scales, within a few days. We were in the early stages of Lisa's radiation treatment so I put it out of my mind and focused on her treatment and other things we had going on back in Dallas after being gone for almost a month.

Another Uncomfortable Step

A few days later I got a call from Dr. Scales's office saying he wanted to see me that week to review the results of the MRI. This was the first time I had real concern that I may have a problem, but even then I was not excessively worried. Lisa asked if I wanted her to go with me and I said no, primarily because I did not want her worried, which she would have if she thought I was worried. I assured her it was no big deal. She had enough on her plate and I dang sure didn't need to add to it.

At the appointment, Dr. Scales explained what the MRI had found. I had a tumor in my prostate. For the next few minutes, as he explained in detail the findings and what they meant, I went in and out of concentrating on what he was saying as a million things flashed through my mind relating to my family and what could be an uncertain health future. However, two things I remember clearly: first, even with this MRI, we could not know if the tumor was malignant; and second, the radiologist rated one area of the tumor as Pirad 5, which meant it was likely malignant. The next step would be to perform a biopsy to remove tissue from the prostate and test it to see if it was malignant. I told myself, *Take the next uncomfortable step, Ron.*

Dr. Scales said having the biopsy was not urgent, and we had plans back at our summer home in North Carolina in late July and early August, so we scheduled the biopsy for August 25—six weeks from the date of the MRI in July. The rest of July was spent with Lisa finishing her radiation treatments and watching her so intensely pray, research, and act.

The cadre of people she found who were promoting a nutritional plan to help fight cancer recommended going vegan, raw, organic, plus very little wheat. This meant no meat of any kind, no bread, and no dairy. Basically, a meal plan of vegetables, fruits, and nuts. Lisa did awesome. I could quickly tell a difference in her appearance and attitude. She lost some weight, even though she has never been heavy, and the meal plan coupled with her daily exercise gave her a slim, athletic look. Her discipline has been phenomenal.

One of my best friends in the world is Dr. Jim Davis from Augusta, Georgia. We met through our golf club in North Carolina and became fast friends, spending many days golfing, trout fishing, and enjoying good meals. Jim is a radiologist so I asked him to look at my MRI results. He saw essentially the same thing as the radiologist who initially read the exam, but Jim recommended I get a radiologist to review it who specialized in prostate MRIs. Through a mutual friend, we found such a radiologist, and he confirmed the initial MRI report: there was a tumor, it could be malignant, and the next step was a biopsy.

Now, a biopsy of your prostate is the type of thing you might wish on your worst enemy but certainly not on anyone you care about! The preparation and recovery process is quite unpleasant, but the biopsy certainly can be necessary. It was time to trust the expert (after confirming with others and doing research), get in the wagon, and let someone else lead this process.

By the grace of modern medicine—in my case a small dose of Valium and a local anesthetic—the biopsy was not particularly painful or, thankfully, memorable. Because of the sedative, Lisa had to drive me to my appointment, wait for me, and drive me home. It took just over an hour. Dr. Scales removed six samples from the tumor area and six from the remainder of the prostate for analysis and comparison. A follow-up appointment was set for September 2.

Having the type of personality that I have, the worst thing in any situation for me is the unknown. This situation was not different, but somehow God put peace in my heart that calmed my spirit. I wanted the result to be good and prayed that it would be, but I was not afraid. My life's journey had been a good one. Whatever happened, I was comfortable that God was truly in control and had blessed me beyond anything my human mind and soul could have ever imagined.

We had learned from Lisa's cancer experience that all cancer cells are not created equal—some are aggressive and some are not—so we prayed and held out hope that mine was not aggressive and could simply be regularly monitored with no further action needed. While I don't want to burst your bubble, let me just warn you that if you ever go to a doctor's appointment and they don't put you in an exam room but instead take you to his office with a desk and chairs, then the news could be disappointing. This happened when we went to see Lisa's doctor after her biopsy, and the same exact thing was happening to us again on September 2 when the nurse said, "Let's go down to Dr. Scales's office and wait for him there."

Have you ever heard the saying, "If one is good, then two is great"? In cancer, not so much.

Dr. Scales has a very good bedside manner but also speaks directly, in easily understandable terms. He entered the room, shut the door, and said, "You have a malignant tumor on your prostate. Every sample we removed from the tumor was malignant cancer, and none of the samples from the remainder of the prostate showed any cancer cells. You have two options: surgery to remove the prostate, or radiation to essentially kill all the cancer cells and likely the good cells in prostate."

He went on to explain something known as the Gleason score, which indicates whether the type of cancer cells found are more or less likely to aggressively spread. A score of 6 and under means not at all likely to spread; 8 and above means very likely to spread. Of course, because nothing ever seems to be black or white, my score was 7, which meant I was at an intermediate risk for the cancer spreading. I thought, *Seriously, God, why is everything always gray?* All that we had encountered lately seemed to be a judgment call. Later that day, spending time in my own thoughts, that still, small voice reminded me that nothing, and I mean nothing, was "gray" to God. Thankfully, Dr. Scales said we did not have to take immediate action. We would monitor for ninety days, check my PSA again, and make decisions from there as to treatment.

And so, another period of the unknown—which we are in as I write this—is testing my faith, my wisdom, my desire, and my character. I need to support Lisa with all I have. I need to love my kids, grandkids, and friends with everything I have in me. And I need to pray, research, and act. I am doing all of this right now, and by the time this book hits your hands we will have taken the action that our prayers and research led us to take.

I strongly desire to live for many more decades, and I want to be healthy during that time. However, if God's plan is different, then I trust him as the ultimate holder of my red wagon handle. He will be faithful to steer me along the right course in his perfect timing.

Acknowledgments

*I*t would be almost impossible to acknowledge all of the people who made this book possible either through their impact on my life or in the fulfillment of my goal to write a book that everyday people could relate to and, I hope, find beneficial to the journey with their "red wagon." However, some people had such an impact that I would be remiss if I did not mention them here.

The late Richard Lewis, Brooks Hamilton, First Baptist Dallas, Bill Quinn, Dr. O. S. Hawkins, Randy Haugen, all my partners and colleagues at Retirement Advisors of America, and finally, The Four Horsemen (you know who you are).

As it relates directly to this book, I must acknowledge Dr. John C. Maxwell and Don Yaeger. Like millions of people around the world, I first learned of John through his books and speeches. I have been fortunate enough to get to know John and be mentored by him over the last several years. Lisa and I love John and his wife, Margaret, and feel blessed to spend time with them at their home playing card and board games or enjoying a great meal at a local restaurant. John encouraged me to write this book, even if it was just for me, and I am thankful he believed enough to have his publishing company take on this project. Don Yaeger was introduced to me by John as one of the world's great storytellers and the perfect fit for helping me write this book. No statement was ever more true. Don has been so faithful to me through this process. He has listened to me laugh and cry as he prompted me to talk about my life journey and then so eloquently put it into the words of this book.

Of course, I hope you enjoy *Life Lessons from the Little Red Wagon*, but mostly my prayer is that it gives you hope in your journey and inspires you, as an average person just like me, to always, always be prepared to take the next uncomfortable step.

My Journey in Photos

Captains of the 1977 Junction City Dragon High School football team were yours truly, Keith Williams, and Roger Adams. The three of us also made All-District and All-County that year.

One might have guessed that I would speak in front of people as an adult. This photo is of me speaking at my high school junior-senior banquet.

Of course, you need to see a photo of some of our Murphy Oil softball team members. The letter I wrote asking for sponsorship and the meeting I had with Mr. Ben Smith turned out to be a huge career turning point in my life.

Our engagement announcement photo that appeared in the local newspaper. That smile of Lisa's is what first caught my eye. I have no idea what she saw in me, but, hey, don't question fate!

My Grandpa and Grandma Martin (my mom's parents) with my three kids in the background (along with my niece). The summer I spent working for Grandpa Martin when I was fifteen was both enjoyable and filled with life lessons I still rely on today.

Although not in the photo, this is from our Amway days when we spoke numerous times at business events around the country. Some of our fondest memories were of our time in this business.

Here he is, the man, the myth, the legend—Randy Haugen. His speech late that night from the Delta Center in Salt Lake City turned me on to the possibilities of purposeful personal development. Randy and I went on several four-wheeling trips with other guys in the Wasatch Mountains.

Lisa said I would never play golf with Billy Florence, a legend in the Amway business. Well, here is proof and we have done this hundreds of times since. This is the golf course near where we both have houses in Cashiers, North Carolina.

My oldest son, Justin, and I have always enjoyed playing golf together. Here we are accepting the championship trophy from our country club's founder for winning a Member–Guest tournament.

No father–son golf life is fully complete until you have traveled together to St. Andrews—the birthplace of golf. This photo is of us near the 18th tee box on the Old Course.

One of the great golf experiences for Justin and me was being able to share a round with one of my mentors and friends, John C. Maxwell, which was also held at the prettiest course in the world: Pebble Beach.

Daniel has always loved all things British, so we traveled with
him to London as his graduation present from high school.
Here he is with London Bridge in the background.

This reminds me of a scene from *The Sound of Music*. Daniel loves our place
in the mountains of North Carolina, and we love it when he is happy.

Daniel's dog is appropriately named Winston in honor
of Winston Churchill. They are inseparable.

Allie Beth and I have a couple of great dad–daughter trips including
this one to NYC as she closes in on finishing college.

Memory-making is what the
Simmons family is all about. We
may forget things but the memories
we make are long-lasting. Here,
Daniel catches a nice trout on
a river in North Carolina.

This is the infamous experience
that made me say, "That's why we
call it hunting, sweetheart" and
Allie's reply (after we saw no game
animals): "I call this a nature walk."
She was outspoken from a very young
age and now it serves her well.

One of my favorite memories is of Allie Beth and I making "cat head" biscuits one Saturday morning when she was just a little tyke.

Of course, now Lisa and I spend a lot of time adoring our grandkids. These three boys—James, Bennett, and Peter—are Justin and Amy's sons. Allie and her husband, Timothy, have two children, but because of her public career, we choose not to publicize any photographs.

One of the benefits of being a state representative in Texas is access
for you and your family "inside the rails." It was special to have Peter
join me on the Speaker's dais before our daily session began.

Representatives Craig Goldman, Drew Springer (now a state senator), me, and
Giovanni Capriglione. We all entered the Texas House together, had some
great times serving in the legislature, and remain great friends to this day.

Governor Greg Abbott signing HB20, the bill I authored in 2015 that changed
the way the Texas Department of Transportation prioritized road projects.
That's me right behind the Governor looking like a Secret Service agent.

Many of my colleagues, along with Lisa and a special needs student, joined
me in a press conference to discuss HB1335, the bill I filed to allow education
options for special needs students. Not everything is rosy; this bill was killed
in the Education committee, which was one of my great disappointments.

My friend and former colleague
Sylvester Turner, a Democrat who
showed me how we can work "across
the aisle" on many items that best
serve the citizens of Texas. One of
the highlights of my legislative career
was serving with Chairman Turner.

She is absolutely as beautiful
today as ever. Lisa has been
by my side every step of the
way . . . even the uncomfortable
ones. We have a lot more to go!

Swearing-in day for me into the Texas House—what an honor and how special it was to have Lisa by my side for this historic event in our lives.

If this doesn't confirm our status as "average" then nothing does! This is the day we were leaving El Dorado to move to the big city of Dallas. Two 24-year-old kids with two babies.

This house is where it all started. Behind us is where I rode my Radio Flyer into history . . . and pain. It was our standard Easter Sunday picture: my siblings—Randy, Rena, me, and Ricky. That's right, all four of us have names starting with the letter "R."